Jacob's Prayer

Caitlin Press Inc.
8100 Alderwood Road,
Halfmoon Bay, BC V0N 1Y1
www.caitlin-press.com

Edited by Harold Rhenisch.
Text and cover designed by Vici Johnstone.
All photos courtesy Lorne Dufour unless otherwise noted.
Cover photograph: David Johnson on the "dome" courtesy Bridget Dan (daughter of David Johnson), photographer unknown.

The Bridge, Old People on the Reserve, Ralph (revised) and The Missionaries were published in *Starting From Promise*, (Broken Jaw Press) and have been included with permission from Broken Jaw Press.

Printed in Canada

Caitlin Press Inc. acknowledges financial support from the Government of Canada through the Book Publishing Industry Development Program and the Canada Council for the Arts, and from the Province of British Columbia through the British Columbia Arts Council and the Book Publisher's Tax Credit.

Library and Archives Canada Cataloguing in Publication

Dufour, Lorne, 1940-
      Jacob's prayer / Lorne Dufour.

ISBN 978-1-894759-33-5

   1. Shuswap Indians--History. 2. Shuswap Indians--Alcohol use. 3. Alkali Lake Indian Reserve No. 1 (B.C.). I. Title.

Jacob's Prayer

Lorne Dufour

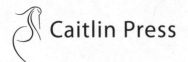
Caitlin Press

Previous page: A storm blowing at Alkali Lake. Photo Vici Johnstone.

Following pages: Children in the classroom at Alkali Lake reserve learning about the wonders of young life.

I dedicate this book, Jacob's Prayer, *to the women who have gone missing on the Highway of Tears, to the lost ones and to their beloved families.*

Contents

Contents cont.

Contents cont.

Foreword

—By Sage Birchwater

Jacob's Prayer is an important story in the literary mosaic that is the lore of the Cariboo Chilcotin. It had its beginnings on a cold, blustery Halloween night in 1975, fifty kilometres south of Williams Lake. Two men, John Rathjen and rancher Martin von Riedemann, lost their lives that night, in a bizarre accident that never should have happened. Lorne Dufour was a school teacher there, in the Secwepemc village of Esket (Alkali Lake). By the grace of God and the quick actions of a Secwepemc man, Jacob Roper, Lorne's life was saved and he lived to tell the tale. This is his story.

The two men who died were both pillars of a community that existed as two solitudes, separated by a narrow, gravel road: the Secwepemc village of Esket on one side of Dog Creek Road, and the opulent Alkali Lake Ranch owned by the Riedemann family on the other.

Alkali Lake Ranch is the oldest continually-operating cattle ranch in British Columbia. It was established in 1861 by Herman Otto Bowe as a stopping house along the Fraser River Trail, the main route to the goldfields of Barkerville until the Cariboo Wagon Road was completed in 1863. Bowe took up the verdant land in the valley previously occupied by the Esketemc people. There was push and shove between the settler armed with deeds from the newly-minted colonial government and the Secwepemc people, who persisted in occupying their ancestral homesites. After Bowe staked his homestead, Esketemc families continued to camp on his preemption whenever he was away. "Old Mr. Bowe would chase the Indians away," recalls Phyllis Chelsea, "and we'd keep coming back." Finally a standoff occurred. An Esketemc woman, hiding her walking stick under her multiple layers of skirts, pretended it was a shotgun. She told Bowe she would shoot him if he didn't back off. "That's why our village of Esket is established where it is," Phyllis says.

Over the years, ownership of Alkali Lake Ranch changed hands several times. In 1910 the historic ranch passed out of the Bowe family when it was purchased by Charles Wynn-Johnson, a British subject who came to British Columbia during the gold rush. Under Wynn-Johnson's tenure the ranch expanded in size, incorporating nearby ranches, until it became one of the largest cattle operations in the province. In 1912 it covered 25,000 acres and ran 1,500 head of cattle. In 1939 the ranch was sold to Mario von Riedemann, who had fled to Canada from Austria with his wife and four children to avoid the Nazi menace. Mario's son, Martin, took over operation of the ranch in 1963.

For over a hundred years there existed an uneasy truce between the villagers of Esket and the owners of Alkali Lake Ranch. It was a bittersweet relationship. Over the decades the ranch grew in size to over 37,000 deeded acres, and provided employment for many Esketemc men and women. During this period, it provided ideal jobs such as cowboying, building fence, haying, irrigating and working the fields for wages. Nonetheless, a persistent struggle for control over resources like water rights and land between the Escetemc and the ranch owners remained. The struggle was framed by the obvious class disparity between the nobility of the ranch owners in their fourteen-bedroom mansion, and the people of Esket living in crowded impoverishment next door.

In the years before the tragic accident, the plague of alcoholism had engulfed the community. Andy Chelsea says: "Drinking only came when S.A. (Social Assistance) came in 1956. Our parents weren't drunks all their lives." By 1970 Andy says everyone in Esket was strung out on booze. "It was so bad people used to call it Alcohol Lake."

What happened in July 1972 is legendary. Andy's seven-year-old daughter Ivy told her mother, Phyllis Chelsea, she didn't want to go home with her because she drank too much. Phyllis took it to heart and promised her daughter she would put down the bottle for ever if she came home with her. She was the first person in the community to quit drinking. Three weeks later Andy followed suit. "I didn't say 'let's do it,'" Phyllis says. "I said *I'd* do it." That fall Andy was elected chief, and for the next year Andy and Phyllis were the only two adults in the community who were sober. Gradually, one by one, other people joined them. By 1975, when Lorne Dufour arrived to teach the Grade 4/5 class, 40 per cent of the adults in Esket had stopped using alcohol.

Martin von Riedemann was only thirty-nine years old when he lost his life in the tragic boating accident on Alkali Lake. He was a man of prominence in the greater community, a founding director of the Cariboo Regional District, and a respected cattleman. It was a gesture of good will toward his aboriginal neighbours that had motivated him to purchase seven hundred dollars worth of fireworks that fall, which he planned to set off on Halloween night from his small boat anchored in the middle of Alkali Lake. Everything went according to plan, until a strong gale-force wind blew up the valley from the Fraser River.

The other victim, John Rathjen, was twenty-nine years old. He was a gifted educator and much-loved principal of the three-classroom elementary school in Esket Village. From Phyllis and Andy's perspective, John was a key figure in the hope they had for their community. "There was a lot of excitement making changes with education," says Phyllis. "There was finally hope. We were going to change the system with DIA (Department of Indian Affairs), then this happened with John."

Prior to opening the school that September, John had been part of a team of educators who ran an inspirational culture and education program at Fish Lake Cultural Centre near Riske Creek, about fifty kilometres from Williams Lake on the Chilcotin side of the Fraser River. Fish Lake was established in 1972 when the chiefs of the fifteen First Nations bands who made up the Cariboo Tribal Council took over a forestry training facility from the Department of Indian Affairs. The federal government had spent hundreds of thousands of dollars constructing the state of the art facility on Department of National Defence property north of Riske Creek to teach First Nations people the ways of the logging industry. Then the government abandoned the project and handed the keys of the facility over to the Tribal Council.

Fish Lake held so much promise in its brief three years of existence. It was a dream come true, a reawakening of aboriginal culture. It brought elders and youth together in an atmosphere of respect and learning. The three aboriginal languages of the region, Secwepemc (Shuswap), Tsilhqot'in (Chilcotin) and Dakelh (Carrier) were written down for the first time, stories and songs were recorded, and traditional crafts were demonstrated and all this information was documented by young aboriginal students. Then in June of 1975, the program came to a sudden halt.

In an attempt to break First Nations' chronic dependency on government handouts, the Union of BC Indian Chiefs made the political decision that spring to reject all federal funding. Their goal was to dismantle the much-despised federal bureaucracy of Indian Affairs. The fifteen chiefs of the Cariboo Tribal Council felt compelled to support this initiative, and overnight the dream that was Fish Lake became a casualty of collateral damage.

As one door closed for John Rathjen, another one opened. With the closing of Fish Lake, he was offered the job of reopening the Esket Elementary School, which had been closed for eight years. Phyllis and Andy Chelsea saw this as an opportunity to realize a cherished dream that the community start taking over its own education programs. Lorne was one of three teachers hired to work in the school, and with John Rathjen he developed individual learning programs for each student. He says a lot of the kids in his Grade 4/5 class had never been taught to read or write. "By the end of the year we got them all going."

There is one more character in this story: Jacob Roper, the man who saved Lorne's life. Eight years earlier, on April 8, 1967, Jacob's nineteen-year-old daughter, Rose Marie, had been found dead beside a gravel road adjacent to a garbage dump. Rose Marie died on the way to a dance at Lac La Hache, forty-five minutes south of Williams Lake. Her naked body was found the next morning, face down in the snow on a gravel road beside the highway. Her neck was broken and her clothes were heaped in a pile nearby. The coroner declared she had likely died of hypothermia. Initially, three young white men were charged with manslaughter for the death of Rose

Marie, then the charges were raised to non-capital murder. On September 11, 1967, a jury of eight men and four women in Quesnel decided that two of the young men were only guilty of common assault, and they were fined two hundred dollars. Charges against the third man were dropped.

Jacob Roper and the entire First Nations community were aghast. So were a growing number of whites, who felt that the justice system had failed by not placing sufficient value on the life of an aboriginal woman. A week after the trial, Jacob and a group of First Nations chiefs met with attorney general Robert Bonner, claiming that the verdict was an extreme miscarriage of justice. However, the court decision prevailed.

Eight years later, on that cold Halloween night in 1975, Jacob didn't hesitate to save a white man's life, as he carried Lorne Dufour's nearly lifeless body from the waters of Alkali Lake to his pickup truck, and drove him to the teacherage next to the school in Esket Village. Jacob knew what to do to treat severe hypothermia. He stripped off Lorne's clothes and put him into a bathtub of warm water. "He kept pouring bucket after bucket of warm water down my backbone until I revived," Lorne recalls.

Jacob says he learned how to treat hypothermia from his grandfather and "all the old Indians." "Water draws out the cold," he explains.

Jacob got practical experience treating hypothermia when he worked at St. Joseph's Mission. "At the Mission, the boys would go skating when the temperature was way below zero. They only had thin socks to wear. Sometimes they'd get really cold. We'd take off their skates and put their feet in warm water. Blood-heat temperature. Too hot is no good."

Jacob says he could have saved Martin's life too, but he

never had the chance. Martin was still alive when he was rescued from the cold water of the lake and whisked up to the ranch house by his family. Still wearing his wet clothes, he was wrapped in a blanket and placed in front of a roaring fireplace, and the doctor was called in Williams Lake.

Jacob says a lot of people make that mistake. "The heat from the fire drives the cold into the body. Water can draw it out, and you wouldn't get sick."

Riedemann died that night from hypothermia as the cold penetrated his body and stopped his heart.

After his warm water treatment in the bathtub, Lorne recovered from his ordeal with no ill effects. "Lorne got up and went back down to the lake to look for his partner," Jacob says. "But there was nothing he could do."

Sadly, John Rathjen never made it to shore. His body was recovered the next day from the lake, close to the spot where Lorne had seen him disappear beneath the waves.

This profound experience changed Lorne's life. "In a way I am Jacob's prayer," he says. "I survived, bought a team of horses and had a family."

In a strange way, Jacob's actions in saving Lorne's life were redemption for any thoughts of hatred and ill will he may have harboured. "By his actions, he got beyond forgiveness. He got in touch with creation. He did it automatically," Lorne reflects. "He did what had to be done. He knew when he was called to do something he could do it. In many ways, Jacob was his own prayer."

from "The Dance"

—William Carlos Williams

But only the dance is sure!
make it your own.
Who can tell
what is to come of it?

in the woods of your
own nature whatever
twig interposes, and bare twigs
have an actuality of their own

this flurry of the storm
that holds us,
plays with us and discards us
dancing, dancing as may be credible.

William Carlos Williams. *Selected Poems,* p. 251
New Directions Publishing

The Bath

Big Jacob poured bucket after bucket of near-scalding water down my spine. Each bucket was a prayer for Jacob, a prayer to his daughter Rose Marie, whose neck had been broken and whose body had been found naked near the garbage dump at Lac La Hache on April 8, 1967. She died in the cold and Jacob knew the prayers of hypothermia. He knew the prayers and I was the one who received the benefit of his dedication and of his hard sorrow.

John was still in the lake when I was in that bathtub with Jacob pouring the hot water. Such a strange night that was when John didn't make it home. Coming from the teacherage where Jacob had coaxed the hypothermia out of my body, the very first object that caught my attention, the first artifact of

Jacob mends his net, 1975.

Lorne Dufour

God, the singular life object that I noticed was a small pile of dog-shit. The most beautiful object I had ever seen, just occupying a small, dusty spot on the side of the road. In desperate times perhaps a jewel of the universe. John would have made endless puns about the whole subject, he would have literally disappeared into a cloud of doggerel, but not that night. That night my friend John disappeared into that deceptive little lake, Alkali Lake.

Jacob became a good friend, and we often shared stories while we enjoyed a cup of tea in my little cabin behind the church at Alkali. One day, Jacob told me that some time after his beautiful daughter had been killed, one of the men responsible had got into drinking again and had strayed too close to Sugarcane (the reserve of the Williams Lake Indian Band). He was found the next morning beside the road, still alive, but minus his testicles. They had been removed by some primitive doctor using the edge of a tin can. I wonder if it was a dog food can? Perhaps it was just a rumour, but life is like that. Death also has its macabre side. Sometimes, though, we do not seem to have any choice in the matter.

Jacob's Prayer

The one in the Book
lived 147 years auld time
helped create his last child
in his nineties
Rose Marie died so young
so terribly at the hands
of the semit (white man)
You entered the darkness

When we met
your name was connected
and when your beautiful daughter
Rose Marie, when she died so young
so terribly at the hands of the semit
you entered the darkness

Later the angel Revenge
presented herself as a knife edge
of snow in October
You could have left me to die
my skin was leprosy white
yet you wrestled with Revenge
wouldn't let me leave

You wrestled all right
but it was me who was touched
me and John two men of peace
and the big rancher Martin
we were all touched

Lorne Dufour

only you didn't let them
take me where the rancher went
you took me home

Many times since then
angels have come for me
yet none of them was Rose Marie
I could not leave
only go deeper
into the forest with horses
where the lost must go
with my lover so beautiful
and all our children
Creole Dan the Mountain Man, Tereina Marie
whose sorrows set us free and Easten
our white knight riding flaming stallions

Angels are messengers yet
something more powerful held me here
more demanding than my gratitude
stirring beyond guilt or regret
You dragged me into the light
the light of the great prayer
torn from your heart

Peace Maker

Martin von Riedemann had gone out onto the lake to fire off some big rockets, giant star blisters and star showers, cannon boomers and umbrella lights. The works cost him about seven hundred dollars, I remember him saying when we had gone to talk to him about the kids at school, about their attitude towards the rich and powerful white rancher, Martin, whose big, baronial ranch clung like a tumor on the side of the reserve.

Originally, the forty-acre Indian reserve, Alkali Lake, was the great barnacle on the side of a ranch, but slowly things were turning inside out. My idea: we just go talk, smoke the peace pipe with Martin; I let him know how we feel and that we think he should attempt to make some contact with the children in the school. We thought Martin might take it upon

The Alkali Lake Ranch in 2009. Photo Vici Johnstone.

Lorne Dufour

David Johnson with his fiddle.

himself to think of a way to start mending fences. We were open to helping him in any way we could. We thought we might ask old David Johnson to play his fiddle when he came to the school. Martin might talk about the great cowboys from Alkali Lake that had worked at the ranch, cowboys like the legendary Sylista, the hockey player on the famous Alkali Lake team, the Indian team that was invited to play against the professional team in Vancouver. Upon attending the games they played in Vancouver, the New York Rangers' general manager Lester Patrick realized he was in the presence of some great hockey players and he offered Sylista a contract for the New York Rangers. Sylista told him he could not accept, because he worked at the Alkali Lake Ranch for fifteen dollars a month!

The ranch still had great cowboys fifty years later: cow punchers like Raybone Johnson who came home from the ranch and past my little cabin each night driving a fine team of black Percherons. He was paid seven or eight dollars per day, and as a family man he bore the humility of being a welfare recipient; a real cowboy doing real cowboy work and still having to line up for welfare.

Hey You People

Hey you people
do you remember David
Old David and his fiddle

Him wandering past
so many homes
down that dusty street
with the old church
anchoring it at one end
and the outdoor
hockey rink at the other

Old David with his fiddle
laid so gently
on his shoulder
For the great spirit
a musical prayer

All the great ones
around him the ones
from before him
and the ones
still to come

Lorne Dufour

Horses grazing in the paddock on the reserve.

The Gesture

I was hoping that the great baron Martin von Riedemann might even consider turning the ranch over to the reserve. It should have belonged to the reserve anyhow. It was the cheap labour provide by the natives which had enabled many Europeans to develop big beef ranches near reserves in central BC, develop them and keep them going on what had been Indian land in the first place. We didn't suggest that; we kind of hoped it might happen. Even the creek that ran down from those eastern meadow lands, meandering right through the existing village known as Alkali Lake Reserve, was legally owned and controlled by the baronial ranch.

Our other ideas were a little less radical. We scheduled a meeting with Martin. John, myself and Ron Fern, the third teacher from the reserve school. We didn't smoke kinnickin-nic, which had been my suggestion. We didn't drink anything stronger than tea, either, but we did talk. We told Martin and his wife that the children were voicing highly negative feelings towards himself and his ranch. He spoke about young hip-pies, who would be stirring up the natives. We spoke about the necessity of finding a harmonious and positive route back to earlier, happier days between the ranch and the reserve. We cautioned that times were changing. Ron argued that the annual Halloween firework display was Martin's means of showing that he still wished to serve the reserve. He would at least continue to entertain them with fireworks on Halloween as he had years before. It's all in the gesture; that was the idea. Dog shit, that's what I thought of the idea of political gestures. The big rancher blowing seven hundred dollars in a fifteen minute show of fire-works for people who work for him for seven or eight dollars per day. Ron was excited. Ron had been a school principal; he knew how to bring people about. He certainly convinced us all. I liked the kinnickinnic idea a lot better: smoke the peace pipe, feel the vibes, communicate brotherhood, or attempt to anyway, and go from there.

*

That night, that Halloween night when John drowned and Martin died of hypothermia and the wind came up sudden, terrible, snapping two-foot spruce up the valley for miles, rip-ping the tops off coniferous trees and tearing the souls of good men like sheets off a clothesline, that night was strange and discomforting with terrible questions. Why did this happen? How come those two men died and I didn't? How come we were in the water with half an inch of snow all around the lake

Lorne Dufour

like frosting, around a blue death stone? I was raised to appreciate the dangers of cold water. I knew not to cross a freezing lake. Most of all I knew that most drowning accidents happen when a person attempts to save someone from an overturned boat when the temperature is around freezing. I prided myself on being a woodsman. My father and both my grandfathers were woodsmen. I knew better. In fact, that same night, during that same incident I remember warning Steve Belleau that he would not likely return should he attempt to swim the eighty or ninety yards and back in those conditions. "I'm not saying you couldn't swim that far, Steve, I am only saying, that you might die out there." That was when we were watching Martin. He was sitting up on the transom of his overturned dingy, hollering for help and waving his arms. We could all see him clearly, even with that devil wind howling like a bitch across the lake. I mean, why did God do that? HE, as the author of life, HE writes a mean novel. HIS stories are unpredictable and often filled with grief and waste.

The closest we ever got to fireworks at Alkali Lake that Halloween night was what the terrible wind provided by blowing through the large bonfire the children and I had built on the shore. We had carefully prepared something that would easily burn, yet we had not prepared ourselves for this. Not one spark emerged from Martin's little rowboat, yet a volcano of screaming sparks was whirling away from our fire and into the darkness.

Dominant Species

The homo sapiens
placed the ungulate
into a most special place

A place from which
only death could provide
an escape.

Another homo sapiens group
spent the day in school
at least a kilometre away.

We could hear the ungulate,
All day long it bellered
it bellered and bellered.

The fear of the ungulate grew.
We could hear it growing.
His howls inspired fear.

Hours after school,
the ungulate became quiet;
we heard it beller no more.

Lorne Dufour

A Place to Die

One evening as John and I were having coffee after a busy day with the children John said, "Lorne, what do you feel about this place?"

It surprised me, him asking me how I felt about Alkali Lake. "Well, you know I love this place John. I think with the creek, the big valley and the beautiful meadows that this is a very special and very beautiful place."

"Yes, but that is all tourist stuff. What do you deeply feel here?"

John was asking me something I could not quite comprehend.

"You mean the people, the Shuswap people?"

"No, not that."

"What are you getting at?"

I remember John gazing at me steadily for a moment before he said, "I think this is a good place to die."

Talk about surprising information. Go ahead and talk about it, but experiencing it leaves a person totally open for a few seconds.

"Are you going whacko on me, John? You have been working too hard."

Reopening an elementary school turned out to be a task that often kept John and me working late into the evenings. Besides, neither of us had committed to true love yet. As busy as he was, as great a teacher as he was, John lived all alone in the large teacherage with its cement floor. I knew he was lonely. He lived like a monk.

One day, one of the ladies told me how "John is a real teacher that time!" I thought she was simply being considerate and polite. She went on: "You all work hard, but John is a real teacher!"

"Yes," I readily agreed. "He is a good teacher and we are all working real hard."

"Oh, you all work hard, but John is a real teacher," she said, for the umpteenth time, then she added: "You, Lorne, you are a hillbilly and the Grade 1-3 guy, that Ron, he's a cowboy!"

Ron had been teaching for many years. Here he had a small class. I think it was twelve students, or less, and by three o'clock he figured his teaching day was over. He had a riding horse, and he would be seen riding about the reserve every once in a while.

I knew that lady was a polite person, but I suddenly realized that she was also a very perceptive person.

"She's as fine a place on this planet as I've ever seen, but there just ain't no such place on this planet as a good place to die, and you better know it, man," I said.

"Ah, come on, it's a feeling, an intuition. Something I know way down deep inside of me."

"What are you saying, John? That you know you are going to die here?"

"Well, I feel that one of us is going to die in this place."

I realized that he was very serious.

"There is no such thing as a good place to die, John. There are places to have picnics, build houses, have babies, dig wells, build shit-houses even, but there are no good places to die; just the right time."

"What do you mean, the right time?"

"I mean I believe that dying has to do with timing and not location. A person might know when he is going to die, the exact second or day even, but never, never the place, John; never the place."

"Maybe you just never had that feeling about a place yet."

"No, I sure as hell haven't."

We practised silence for a few minutes and then John said: "You know something, Lorne?"

"What, John?" I was hoping that he was going to say that he had been putting me on, but I knew him better than that. The rivers that coursed through his veins ran deeper than the oceans.

"I am really happy that I have become your friend."

"What?? What are you talking about now?"

"Seriously, Lorne. You are a special person, and it's really wonderful that I met you."

Coming from John, this was not only unexpected but unbelievable.

"Look, John. I'm just some gypsy hillbilly. Nothing special about me, partner, but I am your friend and you know it. You better also know I don't want to hear any more talk about dying around this place." Glancing towards the back of the church, I added, "It gives me the creeps."

The subject concerning dying someplace sort of creeped me out and so did the almost life-sized Jesus, hanging on his cross like a corpse on the back of the church. I know it is symbolical, but it has been hanging there on the cross for over two thousand years and it has persisted, just hanging there. I would have felt less creepy had the religion placed something symbolical on the back of the church representing eternal life. Something to give us a life, something to promise us joy and eternal happiness, something about promise.

We finished our coffee in what you might call a charged silence. After a few minutes I noticed that John was studying me. A little smile was touching the corners of his lips.

Old People on the Reserve

Two women sit in the yard
one astride a block of wood
and the old grandmother with the
black glasses has brought a chair
to sit upon, a casual throne

They are surrounded by chickens
old cardboard boxes and pieces
of firewood

They hold court while Walter
one of the lady's husbands of
forty years stands before them
talking with his hands in
his pockets

Lorne Dufour

They shape thoughts
with their hands
the blind woman
laughs quietly

Smoke from a bonfire
of debris clouds the air
around them Walter begins
to cough

A dog barks
somewhere in the village
and a rooster crows

When I look again
they have all disappeared
like actors off a stage

Bush Gypsy

I realize now that what John saw in me as something special was how I was going to purchase a team of horses and spend thirty-odd years working with them in the forest. John may have lost his life, he may have lost that part of existence we all get to lose sooner or later, but he is still with us and has been with us as we have lived our thirty-odd years in the woods. While we toughed our fifty-below winters, John has always been with us. He has shared our joy and our sadness and never abandoned us. That time when Prince, that great Clydesdale with whom we moved five hundred loads of logs and with whom we travelled through southern Alberta with

Lorne with his team of clydesdales, Leonard and Dora, 2005.

Lorne Dufour

our gypsy "vardo" wagon, that time when Prince decided to make a break for it and headed full speed down the mountain to run and buck in the field on the back slope of Mt. Ida near Salmon Arm. Diana was on his back, and each time she started to slide over his shoulder—she had no saddle, nothing but a handful of mane like a hand full of lightning—Prince would shift his muscles just enough to set her up safely on his back, and I know John was enjoying that ride with her.

To me John and Prince were working together. Both are among the ancient and innocent creatures of this world. John shared our wild adventures and he brought his great karma to help us survive. We survived being bush gypsies. We survived the BC Forest Service, and that alone presented a challenge John must have enjoyed.

Revelation

This morning
three moose appeared
stepping suddenly
out of the last ice age
thousands of years ago
drifting with December snow

A large cow moose
attending two young bulls
most likely her twins
totally free coming closer
and closer until their freedom
settled into our souls

Their great bells swinging
under prehistoric heads
their innocence rubbing up
against our guilt

We should frighten them
we must introduce them
to humans really strange
in our wheeled vehicle of death
but we didn't, feeling perhaps
they sensed so much more
about us than we
are ashamed of

Lorne Dufour

Man in the Photo

John Rathjen, 1975.

I told the story so often
I memorized all the lies

He was a fool, I told everyone
the man in the photograph

he wanted to save a man
from his own destiny
and that part
was true enough

I said I loved him
and that is also true
I never said how I betrayed him
because nobody would have believed it
I used to tell them how he took me
like a child by the hand to meet God
and while we thought we were agnostics
he did take me to meet God in the Cariboo

I told them how I went along
that last time, scared and hopeful
but I told them I didn't meet God or anyone

But that is where I lied
I betrayed him right there
because I was afraid
The truth is that I did meet God more great
than Saints or Expectation,
more tremendous than fear or hesitation
God was there all right
silent as silence
in His Ruby shirt of flame and I seen him

Just like John figured he would be.

Shick Shicken

Every time I shot a grouse, well maybe not every single time, but many times while shooting at a grouse I thought about sitting on the porch of the little log cabin with John and him telling me he would not always be alive. He just grinned at me.

"Come on, let's go shoot us a chick chicken." It's sort of pronounced shick schicken, the Shuswap word for prairie chicken or ruffled grouse. I had convinced John that I was a crack shot so I got to do the shooting. As it turned out, I missed two chick chickens with the 4/10 from a fairly close range, a shameful performance. As we drove home John teased me about my marksmanship, and I explained how the shot is never a solid pattern, how some guns didn't shoot straight, anything I could think of so he would stop teasing me. Suddenly four or five grouse burst up from the side of the rutted road and flew directly across in front of us at headlight level. Without thinking, John cranked the wheel of his little Datsun pickup and shot across the ditch, hitting one of the chick chickens in midair. He jumped from the truck, and picking the poor grouse up by the neck he shouted, "Ha, ha, Lorne, now that's good shooting."

We laughed all the way home. John made all kinds of puns about the caliber Datsun he was using. After a performance like that, I had to put up with the mad punster and make no bones about it. We drove home and cleaned the bird, guts and all, behind the house.

Tony's Eye

We were enjoying an afternoon field trip when I really met Eddy for the first time. Of course, I had met Eddy in class, but I hadn't had an opportunity to get a feeling for the true magnitude of the little fellow till that day up in the hills south of Alkali.

It was Tony, really, who innocently engineered my meeting with the real Eddy. Up 'til that day, Eddy was a quiet little boy who sat next to Gully and just behind Robert. He was small for his age, so when hockey started he looked gnome-like, because his hockey pants came way down past his knees. We just did not have pants short enough for him.

Tony Johnson, 1975.

Lorne Dufour

Tony was Elsie's boy. He was an artist and a dancer. More than once I saw him come Indian dancing all the way down the street to the school. Sometimes late for school, but never too late for dancing: that was Tony. One day he stuck a big flower to his forehead where his third eye is. At his age, I thought that he did that just for fun. Looking back, I realize that way down deep in the very centre of Tony he understood the sacredness of third eyes and infinite compassion, and understood, even as a ten year old, that he was forever a part of that compassion. I remember him walking up from the creek where we had our sweathouse, our "scelia," with a flower growing out of his third eye.

Opposite: L-R Robert Chelsea, John Johnson, Jimmy Paul, 1975.

The Missionaries
(Salmon Arm '76)

There is a group of them
they come here to the reserve
every summer
they are good people
organize games for the children
sometimes teach them songs about heaven

I met one of them
down by the lake
a little wooden platform
some of the fellows had made
reminds me of a koan
or a meditation station
in a Japanese garden
and the man standing
talking to the children

Lorne Dufour

One little boy, Martin
climbs a tree making monkey noises
beside the missionary.

The missionary smiled
understandingly, do you think,
he asked five-year-old Martin
that you will be able to climb
bigger trees when you are older

(Ah ha, I thought, the heavy
question, the tree of life,
the splintered cross, all that
why doesn't he just relax)
but Martin was younger than me so he replied
Well there are some trees
even you couldn't climb I bet
Oh yeah? jokes the missionary,
are they real big?
No, says Martin, they
are real tiny like
little flowers almost

Oh I see, if I climbed one of them
it would break wouldn't it?
I would hurt it.
No, says Martin, it wouldn't break
it would just bend over and you
would break your head

Bird's Nest

That particular day, Tony was cutting out from the crowd and sneaking back to town when I noticed him. Our little group had sort of hunkered down for a rest on the sidehill, and there goes Tony, just a sneaking from bush to bush like an Apache, so I hollered at him, "Hey, Tony, come back here." Just as I hollered, a small quiet voice off my left elbow said, "Hey Lorne."

Instead of turning to the person speaking my name, I thought it better to catch Tony's attention, so momentarily ignoring the voice behind me I hollered again: "Tonyyy! Tonyyyyyy!"

By this time the entire group was intensely watching Tony the Apache sneak and creep from bush to bush and slip invisibly down the hillside heading back to the village, everyone but the person at my elbow who repeated with a little more

Eddy Johnson and Carlo Ignatius, 1975.

Lorne Dufour

emphasis and some impatience: "Hey Lorne."

Once again ignoring the voice behind me, I called to Tony one last, hopeless time: "Tony, Tony you get back here."

Just as the words were coming out of my mouth, the voice behind me, the quiet voice just off my left elbow said, "Well, fuck you then."

That stopped me cold, because it wasn't the voice of a small, shy, Grade 4 child, but almost a man's voice, expressing impatience at the ignorance of another man. I turned then to face whoever it was who I had offended, and found little Eddy, no higher than my belt, with an angry and hurt expression flashing in his eyes. By way of explaining his swearing at me, the teacher, he said, "I just wanted to SHOW you a bird's nest."

"Eddy, Eddy, Eddy," I said. "Please forgive me. I was trying to catch Tony and didn't want him to go home early."

"I know," he wisely explained. "But I called you three times."

*

Eddy was somebody that you didn't take lightly. Size or no size he meant business.

"Eddy" I said. "I'm sorry. Now let's go look at the bird's nest."

We became pretty good friends, Eddy and I, and I soon learned that Eddy was very impatient with his image. He did not enjoy being small. He didn't like being teased about it either. He had sisters and a brother in another class who were normal sized. I think they must have teased him.

One day I noticed that one of the photographs which decorated an entire wall of our classroom had a hole in it, right where someone's face should have been. I recognized the photo and knew that someone had obliterated Eddy's face. In the picture, there were three or four kids standing together. One of them had no head to speak of. I made inquiries but no one knew who had decapitated the model. Finally I asked Eddy himself.

"I did it." He said in his quiet, matter-of-fact voice.

"Eddy, you cut the head off your own picture? Why did you do that?"

"It's ugly." He said the word deep in his throat and it came out like: "Uk-ley, it's uk-ley!"

"Uk-ley?? What do you mean it's ugly? Eddy what are you talking about?"

"Me. I'm uk-ley. I don't like that picture." He cast his gaze down towards the floor.

"You look at me, Eddy."

He did, looked me square in the eye, asking nothing, giving nothing.

"Eddy, you are a real beautiful little boy. When you smile your entire face lights up like you have a five-hundred-watt bulb in your head and you are beautiful, you hear me?"

I don't think anyone had ever told Eddy about his smile before or even that he was so beautiful. I knew, though, because one day he didn't come to school. Driving in to Williams Lake to see my sweetheart that evening, I met a team and wagon with a big load of hay loose-stacked upon it, coming from the meadow. Way up high in the hay pile I noticed a face.

A big smile lit up that face in that green pile of hay, and it was the most beautiful smile I had ever seen. It was the smile of little Eddy, happy to see me, and happier still to be seen riding on a cloud of good, green hay. Little Eddy, the boy who slept on the floor of a small room in a pastel-colored shack, and here he was, king of the haystack, coming home, pulled by two fine horses after a holiday from school! I have never forgotten that smile.

Lorne Dufour

Diana and Connie Robbins.
Alkali Lake, 1975.

Town Trip

(2003 with Diana, and John in spirit)

Ahead of us rode
at least a dozen ladies
one young man all war paint
stepped back hundreds of years
returning as he always would
astride a fine young horse
and the chief riding
with unquestionable dignity
carrying the Shuswap staff
surmounted by an eagle claw
holding up the sky

Sixteen horses pranced about
while hundreds of vehicles
monster logging trucks, cars, motor-
cycles and motor homes slowed
momentarily to horse speed
then went roaring on
into the machine age
My wagon was filled
men lovely ladies from children
to gentle grandmothers, boys
jam packed with questions

Once I saw a flash of brilliant hair
pure raven-black
the horse dancing sideways
the young rider tossing her head
and for me caught up in that moment
everything was suddenly clear

we returned to town once again
as we always had those many years
we rode the trail that had become paved
in man's attempt to appease
everything that moved
beyond nature's speed
with us the true meaning of horse power
celebrated spiritual eagles circling
overhead, we were no longer
touring on this planet pointing
at interesting reflections
of nature, we had once again
the power

Lorne Dufour

Courage

That year when the rich baronial rancher froze to death and the greatest teacher I ever met, John Rathjen, drowned in that little lake that was locally famous for its annual visit by those strange pelicans, well, that year Alkali Lake Reserve was setting itself up in a glass bowl. Phyllis and Andy Chelsea, the chief and his wife, had begun their anti-alcohol program. It began at ground level and worked up through not only that particular reserve but, like a grassfire, it made a path right through the indigenous population of the entire planet. Alkali Lake Reserve became the first rez that totally devoted itself to

Andy and Phyllis Chelsea with Lorne in 2009. Photo Sage Birchwater.

sobering up and finding, once again, its natural place on this planet. It had become a focus of great power and its true beauty was blossoming daily in the children, who, after lifetimes of despair, were so happy to find their parents and their homes becoming liberated from the control of alcohol.

The Catholic church, the one that had hung a life-sized corpse of Christ on its back wall, that church was being run by a priest with an alcohol problem. Representing the pope, the twelve apostles, and Christ himself, the priest was a drunk. The chief and his council ran him off the reserve.

It was a most powerful move, reflecting the strength the people rediscovered once they turned their backs on alcohol. I knew the story personally, because I moved into the priest's house, that little log cabin where on clear nights, dressed up like Merlin himself, no less, I held astronomy classes. Years later, the reserve made a movie concerning their battle against alcohol. The movie tells their sad and wonderful story, including how they found the courage to face the church and order the priest to leave. He was so embarrassed about his history he refused to play himself in the movie. I enjoyed playing his role in the film *The Honor of All,* which has been seen all over the world. It was a great honor to be part of that movie, but the greatest honor goes to the people who found their own centres and their place on this planet once again.

Shuswap
(Salmon Arm Rez 1976)

Long before the bars opened
the Shuswap left off crossing
the Rockies to follow the prairie
· buffalo in days of old, in days
of old

They finally lost the trail
when they opened the bars
and changed the liquor laws
the best horses left the reserves
sold for fox feed or less
so rich ladies in big cities
could wear fur stoles
to stone churches

Behind the pastel-painted house
standing like snow sculptures
in winter-white silence are
Joe's fine snow-blanket
Appaloosas, mares and colts
and stud their long tails
hemp-solid with burdock
their dark martyred eyes
follow snowflakes

Inside the house
the old chief sits like a statue
before the television that has

been patched up with hockey tape, he has
emptied his house like an irascible
old bear he has chased out all his
children, his soft martyred eyes
stare at the television

He has quit drinking taken to wearing
an eagle feather in his hat brim
they say he only goes out now to throw grass hay
to his horses and a few of the older ones
know they know for what he is
waiting

Lorne Dufour

True Miracles

A few years after the movie *Honor of All* had been made and after it had been taken and played from Australia to the Arctic Circle, I picked up a nice fellow who was hitch hiking from the North. I asked him about his origins, as he was friendly and easy to speak with. He told me he was "an Eskimo" and was on his way to visit people he had met from this part of the country. As we rolled along, he kept glancing at me, until he finally said: "You know, we have met some place."

"No, I don't think so."

"Oh yes, we have," he said. "I never forget a face."

"Even this funny face?"

"Yes, even your funny face. I'm sure we have met some place!" I said nothing, and he continued: "Have you ever visited the Arctic?"

"No," I told him. But I could not make him keep guessing where we had met before, so I added, "No, I have never personally been to that part of the country where you are from, but…" and I turned to look into his eyes. "Have you ever attended one of those rehab programs. You know, the AA (Anti Alcohol) places?"

He looked at me sort of startled for a second, and then a big smile came onto his face.

"AHHH yes, " he said. "That's where we met. You are the priest, aren't you?"

Now, over twenty years since the movie was made, some of the older people from Alkali Lake quite often greet me with some version of "Hello, Father." Usually, I will respond by saying something like, "Hello, my son," or "Go with God, my son," something like that, or I will simply just bless them as a real priest would.

In the movie *Honor of All*, we watch Phyllis pouring an entire bottle of wine down the kitchen sink. Phyllis told me years later that she realized how weak their family had become because of drinking. She knew how important families really are, how fortunate she was to have a strong daughter like little Ivy for getting her to quit drinking, and how lucky she and Andy were to have the family they had. The true miracles of life are not to be denied and sometimes it takes strength for us to face our weaknesses. Phyllis knew that like most of their neighbours the man she had always loved, Andy Chelsea, the father of the children, Ivy's dad, had become a violent alcoholic. The man who could respond with a gentle smile when the doctors told him that unless he quit drinking his liver would slowly turn into a soft pudding, and that it had already started to liquefy. The man she had married, the man who could hunt the moose and fish the salmon, the man who could provide for his family, the man who would become the chief for twenty-two years of Alkali Lake Rez, well that man decided to join her, and little Ivy soon returned to the family she could love. Phyllis still denies that she intentionally decided to get Andy to join her or that they could lead the entire population of their reserve, lead them out into the light of their own pride and strength, but that is exactly what happened.

When John and I arrived at Alkali, Phyllis and Andy had been sober for three years. The entire reserve had become a great dynamo of energy and pride. This was the condition, the real battle scenario that we found Alkali Lake Rez in when we arrived, John Rathjen and I and an old friend of mine, Ron Fern, who had been a school principal for many years on the Sunshine Coast. We were so fortunate to arrive during that great battle. Many had already joined up with Phyllis and Andy, but many were still fighting on the dark side, the side of alcohol.

One of the most controversial ways the chief and councillors fought alcohol was by replacing cash payments with food vouchers. It was called the Food Stamp Program, and many people, whose only income was government-controlled welfare payments, really resented it. One afternoon, one of the unhappy band members, a family man, came armed with a thirty-thirty rifle, and challenged the chief, who was Andy at the time. He threatened: "I will shoot you if you continue to steal our money and just give us food stamps!" He raised his gun over his head, so the chief would see that he was serious.

Andy leapt from his pickup, quickly pulled his own hunting rifle from behind the seat and cranked a bullet into the firing chamber. The man who had come to challenge Andy, realizing he might die, threw his gun to the ground and quickly retreated. The chief picked up the rifle to learn that it was not even loaded and he thanked God that he hadn't shot that man. It was not too long after that incident that the same man joined the war against alcohol and went, as they say, on the wagon for good.

Announced by the Sun

Thousands of spider webs
festoon both sides
of the horse trail
road signs invisible
for those coming
with the light
yet entirely visible
moving into the light

The Priest

Andy and Phyllis visited with me while they were preparing to make *The Honor of All*. I do not know if they thought I could play the priest role because I had lived in the priest's cabin behind the old church, or simply because I was usually ready for anything. When they explained that Father Black had refused to return to the reservation and play out his role in that story, I immediately volunteered to fill the position.

When I proudly brought the finished version and showed it to a group of my relatives in Northern Ontario, my old Aunt Amy, my father's sister, who was sitting in a wheelchair, said, "Oh, Lornie, I never knew that you had become a priest!" She gently smiled at me and said it in a way that made me realize that it made her feel peaceful. I didn't have the heart to disappoint her, but I did try to explain that I was just acting as a priest.

Not long after that, Aunt Amy had a stroke and I went to visit her in the hospital. She could no longer talk. Sitting by her bedside, I must have felt like the priest, because I told her she would be going to Heaven and not to be afraid. She placed her bony hand on my arm and squeezed it, acknowledging her appreciation for my message. May God forgive me.

When the movie was being made, the director explained that the priest was a drunk all right, and that he and the chief there, that Andy Chelsea, were often at odds. My role was to be one of constant contention with him, while hiding behind the holy cloth. Andy is a powerful person and warrior, we had become good friends, and it was difficult to remember that the 'priest' was always to be at odds with him. As we prepared for a shooting, we would have to practice making our faces look

Lorne as the Priest on the movie set of *The Honor for All* talking to the director, Phil Lucas, 1985.

angry or stern. During those preconditioning minutes while the camera men set up, I could never avoid telling Andy something humorous. Despite our roles in the story, our current of connection was never destroyed.

The Bible and the Stones of Infinity

could you imagine jesus as an adolescent
writing poems to some fisherman's daughter
or even playing with model camels
when he was younger
it's not too easy is it
in fact it's downright blasphemous

and then after all those years growing up
amidst joseph's wood shavings and sweat
you would think that when he finally finds
mary of magdalene he'd fall deliriously in love
and hang around for awhile
maybe set up a carpenter's shop near the well
and raise a passel of children

but then it would be just another story
wouldn't it
just another man finding a woman
a lonely lovely woman so great in her generosity
only a blind man could deny it
and the man grips eternity by the innocence
and loses himself in it

Behind the Holy Cloth

He was in trouble, that priest who lived in that little log cabin behind the church. He used to purchase sacramental wine by the case, and he also was not afraid to buy the odd bottle from the bootlegging driver of the local bus, the Dog Creek Stage. He had another problem, too: he had fallen in love with the local nurse. Everyone on the reserve knew that they were lovers. It was becoming more and more difficult for him to continue being a priest. He loved his parishioners and they loved him, but his lifestyle was a problem for the chief and council, who were tackling the problem of alcohol in their community. I mean, how can sobriety be presented by the chief and council while the spiritual leader drinks too much? No matter what the chief suggested to him, the priest was always on the defensive, and he always refused to stop drinking. Finally, the chief and his council ordered him to leave the rez. In short, he was no longer welcome as a resident. He had tried to keep the love he felt for his sweetheart, the nurse, hidden from everyone, instead of sharing that love with everyone, and he was not helping in the big war for sobriety.

Kicking the priest off of the Rez was the best thing the chief and council could have done for him. He married that lovely nurse, quit drinking, and eventually opened up a halfway house for healing alcoholics in Chilliwack. It took great courage for the chief, Andy Chelsea, to finally confront the problems that were keeping the priest from really helping both himself and everyone else. There was a good person hidden away in that holy cloth and Andy expelled him into the world, where the strength of true love could help him learn how to survive.

The Priest's Freedom

To that drunken priest
she hid behind angel smiles
only the blessed could see.
Her kisses were so soft
they were holy, and her love
a miracle only God could not
believe.

To that lovely nurse,
he had filled her dreams,
made her weep woman tears,
something she might have forgotten.
Only the mass wine was drowning them
and the holy cloth, its costume.

The chief and his council
exiled the priest and his lover
sent them where alcohol reigns
and true love is hidden
in the land of shame
while in this the war village
only the strong could live
and fight for their freedom

Bless You

I must say, I did enjoy being a priest, but it was difficult watching the people of Alkali relive the sad experiences that alcohol had dragged them through. As I played the priest, I would try to lift some of the actors back into the light of sobriety. In one scene, a funeral scene, one village member had been killed in a fight at a bar in Williams Lake. His lover and wife was up front near the casket, as she had been in real life almost ten years before. I could see that she was reagonizing all the suffering she had originally gone through. While I somberly swung the great incense lantern forwards and back, I managed to catch her eye and winked at her. Whispering so that the sound system would not hear my words, I told her "Let the sorrows go now. You already went through this great sorrow. You are clean now." She glanced at me, and let out a sigh, which most likely pleased the poor man she was missing.

Another scene depicts the priest speaking to the parishioners as they leave the church. Since it was taken from a distance, we were actually allowed great freedom with the script. There I enjoyed swaying back and forth, as if drunk from too much consecrated wine, and speaking with the women. Pretending to be half cut, as it were, I would try to set up dates with the ladies. In the final cut of the movie, one of them is suddenly putting her hand before her mouth to hide the big smile she could not control as I, the priest, hustled her.

Lovers on the Rez

The priest and the nurse were not the only lovers discovered on the rez while I lived there. Quite often, some of the ladies would visit me and my sweetheart when she spent the weekend with me. One time we will always cherish was a visit in the middle of the night from one of the ladies who never hesitated to share her love with us. She had been drinking, and was feeling very sad and guilty, and jumped into bed with us before we could evolve into proper hosts and offer her a cup of tea. Through her tears, she explained that she had just had a fight with her husband. In fact, she had swatted him down like a fly, yet she knew that she did love him. The poor woman was in tears, and of course we were hoping that her lover was not beaten up too seriously. We climbed out of our bed, which was obviously a very special place, as it was where the priest and the nurse had often slept. We made her a cup of tea and while she drank it we learned that her husband had not been too seriously smashed up, and that it hadn't been the first time she had let her temper take over her emotions. We visited with her for a long time, until all her love flooded over her shame and she emerged as a caring partner who was anxious to return to her lover just to hold him in her arms. She left us in the dark, but the next day we met her and her husband, obviously happy to be together, and heading out to the meadows with their team of horses.

A few years after the movie had been made, my sweetheart and I and two of our small children attended a wedding. We were about to enter the church just behind an elderly native couple. Being elders, they did tend to speak a little louder than normal and Diana heard the gentleman saying, "There's the priest! And he's got a wife and some kits now!"

Our People

Elsie Johnson was a beautiful woman, a dancer and a woman of substance and vision. Sometimes Elsie would take a little drink and maybe she would dance, but her dance was never the mindless foolishness of some wino, never. It was very emotional and sincere and spiritual. Her family were the artists, the dancers and carvers and poets of her people. The Shuswap had never been a war people, so her ancestors had been the true aristocrats of the tribe. Elsie liked us, and we were very proud of that. She danced once to drive the "semit" out of me, and it was very difficult for her but she did it and I was spiritually cleansed in her tears. Of course, that lovely grandmother of twelve, or so I imagine, well she did have designs on my body, a fact that caused me some humility and embarrassment. She was such a fine woman, I felt that she would have never forgiven herself had I the seminal courage to take her in my arms and love her as such a woman needs to be loved. Not only that, but her husband, a legendary, powerful person, whose nickname was Raybone, was definitely not someone to cause anger in, and that is a fact a decent man has to accept.

Elsie did, however, take me into her heart, and like all the good people at that place, she held me there, safe and happy, as a person will hold her infant daughter or son to shield them against the brutality of life. Above all else, Elsie was a shield. Like a muskox, she naturally placed herself between the people she loved and the dangers of life. That was her real gift, to be a protector; like all true artists, she placed the gifts of her talents in protective, magic circles around her people.

One time, I remember she and another lady friend, Celina, were talking about the difficulty of survival.

"Those damn semit." Now, semit is the word for "white" person in Shuswap. Elsie must have noticed me flinch with guilt. I knew the word and its connotation. She quickly turned to me and said, "Not you, Lorne, We don't mean you. You are not one of them. It is a word to mean *them* and not you or John or anyone we know here." It was a lesson for me: a person could be a white man but not a white man, or his skin might be white but his soul was the same as the soul of any good person. I recall once referring to myself as "white eyes," to be promptly reminded that MY eyes were blue-grey and not "white eyes" at all. That deep current of acceptance and reassurance stirred through every discourse and communication we had with so many of those good people.

Before I Ever Saw a Muskox

Sometimes we should all remember
the distant gentle thunder
when muskox cross the wintery
tundra, something from the deep
echo of who we are together

We should remember the warm
safety of the inner circle
the great and the strong
all around us when
nothing could hurt us,
falling asleep in
someone's arms

Before I ever heard the tears
of the great muskox fall
silent as the snow I heard
a mother laughing somewhere
I saw a lonely boy
with a hockey stick
playing in a parking lot

Read a poem
about an elephant
and in the absence of just
one desired kiss I saw
my lifetime slowly pass
like lazy snowflakes   tumbling
across the steamy breath
of the great and gentle muskox

Lorne Dufour

Lorne Dufour

Personal Power

It was never difficult to find either powerful people or powerful creatures at Alkali, like the big raven that came to us early in the morning. The rising sun revealed the blue-green shimmer of its darkness, which is very akin to the iridescence that glows through the hair on the people living at Alkali. The raven helped me to realize that when Noah released the raven from that big ship he found the sacred land, a land even more holy than any religious land could be. It was sacred because so many understood its power and so many had been marked through the inner light of that power.

When we spoke to the rancher, however, we learned that the white man dismissed us as fellow white men living with and among Indians. We had ceased to think of ourselves like that whatsoever. Because of the deep spiritual magic in the people who loved us there, the concept of "our people" was much larger than nationality or culture. "Our people" included everyone whose heart could understand that should a small child wander out into the village street any day of any week, within minutes another child would be there to watch over that child. Our people were a free people with their love and their lives. They knew the secret of personal power: you do not squander it; you do not throw it away pointlessly; you share it in such a way that more power is created. Personal power is not poured into the black holes of human greed. Personal power thrives and grows among people of power.

Previous pages: Racing at school. Jimmy Paul is in the lead with Alfred Harry and Corrine Johnson on his heels, 1975.

Sandhill Cranes Again

For a full hour
flocks of cranes came chortling
into a rendezvous place where
the sky was a neighbourhood
I counted fifteen flocks
some four or five hundred strong
they would join up with another
group and begin spiraling,
spiraling into a deep twister
climbing faster and faster
From my vantage point
they individually moved so quickly
they changed into shreds of some
ancient language, a spiral of words
becoming an indelible mandala
A giant visual corkscrew twisting
into a place where power awaits them
and just as sudden as they first appeared
they formed a perfect hippy formation
a giant V for peace brother
and hauled ass for warmer places
leaving me feeling like part
of the wind

Lorne Dufour

Don't Give it Away

One day the chief, Andy, and I were left in charge of the polling station on election day. It was a long, boring and very tiring experience, yet while I was growing more and more weary Andy showed no signs of fatigue. When we finished our shift around 6:00 p.m., we stood for a moment gazing across the wide valley towards the hills on the other side. The hills that lifted right into the sky.

"We should run up that hill, Lorne."

"Andy, are you kidding? I'm beat. It's been a long day here. I just want to go home and make a cup of coffee and relax, man."

"Well, I'm going for a hike."

"Aren't you tired, Andy? You have been here all day too."

"No, I could run across to that hill and run right to the top right now."

I never doubted for a second that Andy could have done it, either. He was about my age, slightly overweight, but an immensely powerful man. In fact, he was like a bear.

"How do you do it, Andy? I mean, how come you are not totally exhausted right now?"

"I just don't give my power away."

This was coming from a long ways back. In the white culture we are taught from a very early age to devote our time and our lives to earning a living. People hold us in scorn if we are not totally committed to working and earning a living. We are expected to exhaust our bodies in some service or another that will not only help society but will earn us a living: earning our way, being paid for our work and for the time it took us to accomplish it. Indeed, a totally exhausted man is one who has most sincerely done his part to earn a living. "No grass growing under that old son. He worked himself right into an early grave, and more the power to him, too."

Andy was coming from a totally different point of view. A different way not only of looking at life but of living. For Andy, totally exhausted, totally wasted was not a state to be respected so much as a condition to be pitied. It showed a man who didn't have the common sense to keep real personal power, which he could then share. A man that exhausted his reserves of personal power for money was obviously very foolish and misguided. If you couldn't run two miles across a valley and run right up a small mountain after spending ten hours governing a polling station, then you had something to learn about living.

Lorne Dufour

Searching for Meteorites

It was an accident
not the meteorite
but looking for it
And running into
that bear
not my accident
mind you
but his

Two totally different
species, or so he thought
coming together
way up high
on the ancient rim
of some volcano
which probably blew
in dinosaur days
sixty-some million years ago

Long before drive-in theaters
or newspapers with political heroes
caught in the captions
of their generosities
way, way, way before
the planet was ruled
by mankind
when bears were one
of the natives

Running into him
damn near caused
mutual heart attacks
Limbs were snapping
small trees cracking
and him all loud and growly

Similar to old marriages
pressed into unexpected
actions of total
anxiety Thank God
I had packed the three
hundred mag that day
As it was I almost
shit my pants and him
the poor fellow twice
my size or greater and so frightened

Everything grew funeral quiet
and I began looking around
deciding on one direction
found him at least fifty feet
up into a large Douglas fir
that had once witnessed
only Indians slipping by
before ships had arrived
and Columbus beat the competition
to the planet's paradise

Peeking down at me
infant-like having

Lorne Dufour

met the Terrible Monster
one of the humans
a great Columbus mustache
and carrying one of those
thunder-sticks
rationalized like Victoria's Secrets
sweet asses in thonged bikinis
and guns that will kill us

A totally misfired species
and him: innocent bear so lonely
holding onto the trunk of a tree
thinking all in a second
about his mom and clinging
to his memories

I felt so happy
to see him so high
I greeted him and
left the scene
what a face
looking down at me
what an expression
sure be great
if we could become
reborn bears
flipping galaxies over
discovering new planets
like the ants
building
infinite
cities

I won't ever forget the first time I saw the Alkali Lake Rez. God, but it was beautiful. From the vantage point of a big hill half a mile away at the north end of the village's large grass meadow, it seemed so small to me. One main dusty street with the church set up at one end and the school at the other. All those little pastel-coloured houses lining both sides of that street with a few sort of stealing away down past the school and up past the church. There was a creek as blue as blue birds. It meandered from the northeast, went through the border of a large green hayfield then down below the church and further down off of that benchland into a stand of willow, to disappear as it worked its way towards the lake. A horse corral like a beautiful postage stamp at the north end, and then at the south end of the village the bench bevelled down towards the small lake: Alkali Lake, itself. The gigantic ranch with its hayfields further west of the lake and its buildings and barns closer to the creek to the north.

I thought the ranch was confined to the west side of the main road but later learned that the ranch owned land almost all the way down to the next reserve, Dog Creek, which was across almost thirty miles of grassy meadows shouldering the Fraser River.

One day I overheard a visitor to the reserve talking about a group of fellows, guys and girls, who had just walked home from Dog Creek Reserve, some twelve miles. "Hell, those people headed out to pick up people at Dog Creek. When the car broke down, they just bailed out and left it and walked the rest of the way home."

What a beautiful, and peaceful and free, picture that evoked in my mind. Imagine simply abandoning a car, one of our technological wonders: abandoning it in the woods, slamming the door and walking away. It is as refreshing as spring rain.

"So what's wrong with that?" I wanted to know.

"Oh, nothing's wrong, I suppose, but if they had more drive, more determination and aggressiveness, they would have made sure they made it to town and did what they had originally set out to do."

"You have a point there," I agreed. "But perhaps those people don't have such well-defined goals. Maybe, for instance, it is just as important for them to spend three hours walking together down the country road, as it is to be driving into town to spend some money. I mean, they might be listening to the birds sing and having a really good time walking."

The person did not seem totally satisfied with that explanation, and I never did know if he really ever appreciated what had happened that day. Cars, trucks, computers, all technology, can keep on evolving full bore, be that as it may, but sometimes it requires strength and courage and real true determination to walk away from the wonders of technology and allow ourselves to return on foot.

Anchored

Sometimes a jet will peel
across the entire sky
the horses don't bother
looking at it don't realize
it might be full of bombs
it might be full of promises
full of hugs and kisses
they don't seem to care
What we do is so important
every single footstep counts
nothing can be wasted
nothing can be done
simply for the sorrow
having lost a great horse
nothing seems to matter
we must work diligently
anchored to the earth
our path was pre-chosen by horses
they threw a line overboard
centuries and centuries ago
and we ended up tied to that line
they tied their hearts like ships
to our hearts like anchors
and now we watch the jets
but the horses don't bother
they watch only us
and we matter so much

Lorne Dufour

There were many visitors to Alkali that year. Some of them left ripples of laughter in their wake. Once someone arrived with a poster. It grandly advertised that a small combo of jazz musicians would come and give a concert at the school on Friday. Jazz at Alkali! Not just ordinary jazz, like small town guys jazzin' round, but real New York Jazz. Well, almost real New York Jazz. Thelonius Monk wasn't there, but the musicians were authentic jazz musicians on tour, and someone had encouraged them to visit a small and remote Indian reserve in Central BC.

Now there were twelve or fourteen people living at Walter and Theresa's, right across the yard from my place behind the church. Walter and I had become good friends and I often visited them. Usually, someone was playing records or listening to the radio. Musical tastes among the adults as well as the kids ranged mostly from country to rock, and that is *basic* country and *basic* rock and roll. Elvis was still number one, and Suzi Quatro could be heard hammering out her raunchy lyrics late into the clear, starry, Cariboo night. Jazz at Alkali??

Well, if the musicians were true music lovers, then their trip just might go over, but if they were up on jazz and down on everything else, then well…who knows?

Sure enough, Friday, just after lunch, the three jazz musicians arrived in a rented car: a bongo player, one base fiddler and a saxophonist. They had only been playing for a few minutes, when those of us who had haunted the coffee houses in Vancouver during our university days realized that the gig time, or the big time, had finally reached Alkali. We studied the audience, which sat there quietly studying the musicians.

This atmosphere of waiting continued for ten minutes. I realized that the children were waiting for the musicians to stop warming up and to break into some good rock and roll.

The man on the bass fiddle seemed to perceive this, too. He figured he should give the locals a little chat about the state of music in Paris. He opened with a provocative statement, how provocative he could never really know, but he waited until absolute, coffin-making silence had descended on the audience and he said: "Rock and roll is DEAD. This is JAZZ, and in all the big centres of culture, like New York, San Francisco, Chicago, Montreal, Jazz is the music people listen to

Lorne and the kids in the classroom: Kelly Johnson, Tony Johnson, Robert Chelsea, John Johnson, Willy Johnson, Lorne Dufour, Douglas Robbins, Jimmy Paul, Wilma Dick, Deno Chelsea and Ralph Johnson.

Lorne Dufour

now. It is what we call an 'upbeat tempo.'" Turning to his friend Charlie, he said, "Take her away, Charlie."

Charlie turned out a few licks on his sax, but failed to take the kids away with him.

Rock and roll is dead?? The kids' eyes were flashing that question towards us teachers, who they knew and trusted. This was pretty heavy. I don't even think that Elvis had died yet, and even if he had they just couldn't ever possibly comprehend how such moving music could just up and die like that. Music ain't like a cat you like, which when it just up and dies on you, you get another cat. Rock and roll is on records, and so long as you have records the music isn't going to die. Besides the little Alkali Lake rock group could play most of the greatest rock and roll songs, and more kids would learn how to play guitars and sing, so how could the music die? I could see the questions in their eyes. Just who are these guys, Lorne? We like the dreams but what in the world are they talking about?

The concert wound itself down off of the Eiffel Tower of culture and things got a little quiet in the basement of Alkali Elementary. The musicians smiled at the applause we sort of coaxed out of the kids and they began packing up their instruments. Quite a few adults had attended, including the Alkali Eagles, the rock and roll band, and old David Johnson the fiddler, but no one spoke with the musicians. Leading a silent, almost funereal-type procession, the combo carried their instruments upstairs and out to the waiting rental car. We teachers, acting in part as the genial hosts, shook hands with them and thanked them for coming, reassuring them about the acceptance of their music by the kids. We knew the kids loved anything different and loved any form of music, so that part was easy, but we didn't tell them that their doomsday message about rock 'n roll had fallen on deaf ears.

The car slowly rolled down the single street and past the church. Turning down by Elsie's place, it crossed the creek and began to disappear forever, when suddenly one of the children came running out of the school basement, stirring up the wide circle of stunned people who stood silently in the dust of the departing automobile.

"Lorne! Lorne!" It was Willy. "What is it, Willy?"

"This! They forgot this!" Willy held up the bow, which the bass player had forgotten.

Automatically someone in the crowd shouted, "Quick! Quick, catch them up! Quick!"

Before I knew it, Willy and Ralph and Kelly and I were leaping into my little Volkswagen and screaming off down the road after the musicians. We knew the road better than they did and caught up with them inside of a few miles. I pulled up alongside just like on TV, and the kids were waving frantically out the window. The big rented car pulled over and we stopped in front of them. We all got out of the car and ran back to them.

"What is it?" said the driver, looking a little anxious.

"This!" announced Willy, as he swept the bow like Sir Galahad sweeping out his great sword, "This!" he repeated, brandishing the bow. "You forgot this," he humbly added.

The three men in the car exchanged cautious glances, and I felt a communal sigh of relief escape their chests as the driver reached for the bow and said, simply, "OHHHAHH!"

The Dog Catcher

Alkali didn't have any dog catchers. Round about every time there got to be too many dogs around chasing Theresa's chickens or ripping up too many garbage cans or running the deer too much in the hills, somebody would put up a notice that all the dogs better be tied up before Tuesday next, because the loose ones would be shot. I made sure John's dog, Daydog, was tied up that Tuesday. He was a good little partner and hung around with me for a few years after John left him with me.

One time I was sitting on the floor in class, the kids sitting in a big circle all around me as I read them a story. I cannot remember which story I was reading, but Daydog worked his way through the big circle and got as close to me as possible and never took his nose out of the book while I was reading. One of the students asked me if the dog could read, if Daydog could read, and I said it sure looks like he can, but way down deep I knew that John loved books and Daydog remembered John with his face in a book. I thought that Daydog was thinking that perhaps through the book he could find John again. I did not tell the kids that, though.

The day the notice went up concerning dogs, I thought of Ralph and his big, powerful, white shepherd dog. That dog commanded respect from man and beast alike. One time, when the class was on one of its frequent field trips, Raph's dog decided to eat Daydog.

"Lorne! Lorne!"

"What is it, Eddy?"

"Come quick! Ralph's dog is killing Daydog!"

We ran to the spot where the fur was flying and the dogs were snapping and growling and shrieking. I knew it was

Daydog doing the shrieking, because he was not a fighter. I knew the big white shepherd dog was doing the low growling, because you could always tell real easy that he was full of business, no fooling around.

I ran into the middle of the fight and dug my hands into the deep fur on his neck and dragged all hundred-plus pounds of him off of Daydog and flung him back. Instead of rushing back in to finish the kill as most dogs would have done, this particular fellow turned full square and looked me right in the eye. I noticed, for the very first time, that there was a lot of wolf in this animal. I also noticed that during that breathless interval he was facing me as a possible enemy. For a second nobody made a sound. Even Daydog stopped whimpering and watched Ralph's big white wolf dog. Even Ralph was just watching, and I understood that Ralph knew his dog so well he didn't know what the dog might do. There was a serious possibility that the big fellow might just decide to tear my throat out. He was absolutely fearless, and behind his yellow eyes thoughts were racing like small clouds driven by a high wind. Before he could latch onto one of those thoughts, I said with a voice as fierce as I could muster: "You get out of here!" As I said this I scooped up a handful of snow and showered it into his face. He looked at me for another moment, as if he wanted it to register that the puny human teacher did not constitute any kind of threat to him, then he turned his muscled shoulder and ran off.

All the kids started talking at the same time, revealing the deep relief they were feeling. I turned to see Ralph breathing a sigh of relief as he looked at me.

"Quite a dog you have there, Ralph."

"Yeah, he is pretty tough."

"He'd make a good sleigh dog, Ralph. Ever try him?"

Lorne Dufour

"Yeah we hooked him to the toboggan sometimes. He pulls real good."

"I guess so. That big critter could pull like a Clydesdale"

I began to take particular notice of that dog after that, and I saw him every day or so. He usually walked to school with Ralph. Often I'd see him running back of the school up towards the wild country.

Tuesday rolled around. I had tied Daydog to the porch of my little cabin. We were quietly working away in our class when gunshots began happening down the street away from the school. The kids rose as one and rushed to the windows. I had been tying Daydog every day since the notice a week before and had forgotten about the possibilities.

"What is it? Who is doing the shooting?" I thought that maybe some of the men were lining up their sights for hunting.

"It's the docks, they are shooting the docks," one of the girls informed me. She said "docks" sort of dragging out the hard c sound. Ron, the teacher doing Kindergarten to Grade Three, came into the class then and said that a wounded dog had run down into the basement of the school. Ron had a gun with him, so he and I, accompanied by all the kids in my class, ran around to the back of the school and looked down the cement stairs to the basement. There was a sad and runty little collie dog huddled near the door. Blood marked his trail across the yard and down the stairs, so we knew he was hit bad.

"Here" said Ron "You finish him."

"Whose dog is it?"

Ultimately we had to send this little collie on his way; I was hoping he didn't belong to one of the kids in our class. Ralph's brother Kelly told me, "It's Gully's dock, but she don't want him, didn't tie him up!"

I couldn't see Gully just then, so I ordered the kids back to the classroom, and taking careful aim I placed a shot directly behind the left ear of the pathetic, wounded creature. I aimed behind his left ear but I must have missed because that poor little guy began snarling at me. The animal had courage, and Ron who was looking over my shoulder said something encouraging like, "Christ, but I can't stand a man who can't shoot straight!"

"Never mind the bullshit, give me another bullet."

He handed me another little brass-shelled .22 bullet. This time I walked right up to the dog, placed the gun to its ear and pulled the trigger. It died instantly, without a move, it just stiffened and died. We carried it up out of the basement and hauled it back of the building, where we would later bury it.

"God," I thought, "poor Gully. She will be broken-hearted."

I hurried back to class and busied myself at my desk, afraid, almost, to look at Gully.

Kelly came up to my desk. "Dit you shoot him, Lorne?"

"Yeah, he was wounded real bad. Was the only thing I could do."

Kelly did not respond. He stood quietly beside my desk as if he had another question, or perhaps he was letting me arrange my thoughts before his next question, so I asked him, "How is Gully taking it?"

There was a slightly mischievous glint in Kelly's eyes, which I mistook, due to the excitement and everything. Kelly replied: "Real bat, Lorne. Real bat." He shook his head dramatically and walked solemnly back to his desk.

"Christ, why me? I never shot the darn dog in the first place," I was thinking, when little Gully came up to my desk. I looked into her soft brown eyes.

"Hey, Lorne, I mate you a picture." She handed me a lovely painting she had made for me. It was a scene of the village with clouds rolling by the far hills, little houses down in the valley and a big happy sun shining overhead. As I studied it, I realized that she had begun to paint it when we had gone out to kill her dog.

Ralph never came to school the next morning. Kelly told me he was at the dump.

"At the dump?"

"Yes, Lorne."

"What is at the dump? I mean is it more important to go to school or to go to the dump, for God's sake?"

"Hiss doc. Hiss doc is at the dump. Somebody shot him yesterday!"

"Ralph's dog, the white dog?"

"Yes."

"Ralph told me he tied it up yesterday. I asked him."

"Yeah, but the doc got loose from it."

Ralph didn't come to school that afternoon, either, although the inspector dropped in that afternoon.

"Where is Ralph Johnson today, Lorne?"

"He had to go to the dump."

"The dump?"

"Yeah, seems someone killed his dog. He really loved that dog. I guess he went and got him and buried him someplace."

Ralph was pretty quiet around school for a while after that. Real quiet.

Ralph
(Alkali Lake Reserve)

Yesterday he went
to the dump
the prayer dump
of garbage

He found his dog
that was shot
he buried him

He didn't come back
to school that day
and the inspector
came and the principal

Lorne Dufour

(knowing there is a slim
possibility that God
may not exist at all)

They spoke of
irresponsibility
lack of discipline
how children must learn
to be on time

The butchered vision
of reality
cluttered with the ugliness
of its power

As if that empty equation
of time, of punctuality, of
punch-the-clock
responsibility

As if it could match
even for one simple second
just one cool nuzzle
of one dog's nose

In one boy's hand
on one Indian
reservation

Previous page: Astronomy lessons. Ralph Johnson (in the goggles), Joe
Paul, Jimmy Paul, Willy Johnson, John Johnson, Douglas Robbins and
Robert Chelsea.

The Meadows

A mile or two east of the village, a rutted road wanders back into the hills. If you followed this road you would come to a creek. Crossing this creek, you could pick up your trail again, your trail running due south towards a small lake. Just before the lake, you would come upon the first "meadow." The meadows are large, natural fields that wind themselves like giant prayer beads back into the hills. Each meadow was owned and managed by a different family and most had one or more log cabins on them. Some had old-time cabins with sod roofs shielding them from rain and snow. When I was at Alkali I learned that most of the families would hook up their teams to their wagons or Bennett-buggies, pile the groceries, the rifle, the grandparents and the kids onto the back, and with mom and dad and a cousin or uncle regally enthroned on the car seat, appropriately mounted, they would disappear for several months each year "up the meadows."

How special and wonderful to be able to live like that: spend your winters down in the village so the kids could attend school, then head on out to the meadow for haying, trapping, fishing and hunting for the rest of the year. I suggested that they cut the school year down to the four worst months of the winter and have gypsy tutors to go and live with different families during the rest of the year. A roving tutor could go from meadow to meadow on horseback or with a team and wagon, and keep the kids tuned in as it were. What a good life. The school board didn't go for the idea, though, and encouraged the different families to settle fairly permanently in the village and use the meadow homes as sort of vacation areas, much like white people who have a cottage by the lake. Very few people

93

ever drove trucks or cars up that deeply rutted road into the meadows, although it was not forbidden. Everyone seemed to respect the serenity and peacefulness of the meadow too much to desecrate it with carbon monoxide and loud noises, so the usual method of transportation was the horses and the Bennett-buggies.

Every family had at least one good team of horses or one or more riding horse at Alkali Lake then. The men used horses to break ground and cultivate their community garden. They used their horses for harvesting their hay and hauling it home, and they used their teams to visit about and to run down to the store which nestled up against the fence of the great Alkali Lake ranch. Some of the younger men, the more aggressive men, were talking about bringing in tractors to do their farm work. I prayed that the old timers would never allow that to happen. When people lose contact with horses and horse power, they lose something so intangible, so important it can never be regained or replaced. Every time a person harnesses up a horse to do something he could do just as easily with a tractor I always know that person is making a prayer for this planet.

Previous pages: Walter Paul and helper delivering firewood in Alkali in 1975.

Sweat Bath

black womb
of hot steam
sweat and ribs
of white willow
make me once again
fresh born

let hot breath
of mother earth
penetrate to
my tired bones

my bones are full of fire
and all my blood
bubbles in my veins

make my heart clean
make the smell of money
leave my hands
let the stink
of greed leave me
once again

black womb
of fear and joy
push me out
into world

Lorne Dufour

Building a Garden

Alkali Lake had begun to lift itself into the modern world. The people of Alkali had developed a large garden, which met many of their vegetable needs. They set up a productive sawmill, which employed some of their families. They developed a logging company and bought skidders and loaders, which provided employment for yet more families. Irrigation systems had been designed and installed by the members of the village hockey team, and had become so important to economic survival. Research had begun on the Shuswap language, so that it could never be forgotten. Local people like Freddy Johnson, Celina Harry, and Bridgit Dan became teachers at the school. As Andy Chelsea recently explained to me, "One of the most difficult challenges we faced, the challenge that persists to this day, is to finally realize that we are all equals on this entire planet."

Horse Power

Everyone used horses for everything at Alkali. No one was adding to the pollution of the planet. Everyone was, in fact, living a prayer that the planet would continue to blossom. I hoped that would never change. In my life after leaving Alkali, I've tried to keep the prayer alive.

I recall once that a group of us men were talking about the wild meadows.

One of the men introduced the idea of trail bikes. "Yeah, me and Doreen are gonna get trail bikes."

"Trail bikes?" I inquired. The thought was totally abhorrent to me.

Lorne and Michael Underhill breaking the land with Andy and Prince, Enderby, BC, 1980.

Lorne Dufour

"Yes, you know, Suzukis or something like that, Enduros or Hondas."

"What in the world would you want with a trail bike?"

"Well, for one thing, we could buzz up to the meadows in half an hour or so. Now if we want to go up there it takes most of the day."

"Good God, man, but it's supposed to take most of the day. Don't you realize that?"

He looked at me for a full moment, trying to figure out where the hell I was coming from.

"What do you mean, it's supposed to take half a day to get there? Haven't you heard about 'progress?'"

"Look at it, man" I said. "You get motorcycles to go up to the meadows, pretty soon you will be moving hydro generators up there to run the televisions you will want to bring in. First thing you know, twenty years or so down the road, you will wake up one morning and look around. All you can see is junk. Once your life was subtle and strong and clear, but all of a sudden you have cluttered it up with so much junk you don't even know what you are doing anymore. You turn to your wife and you say, 'Those damn whitemen, the semit. Look what they did to our lives. They filled our lives with junk.'"

The man stared at me for a moment, then turned and walked away. I felt that I should have been more diplomatic, more sensitive, less eager to warn him about the pitfalls of technological wonders, but I knew I was right and so did he.

Star Horse

Full moon fills eastern sky
pin point stars appearing
silver sparks in the deep blue
blanket

Darkness dismissed
going to places
welcoming it
like doubt
greed
war

I mounted our beautiful horse
rode down the homeward trail
wondering if great spy satellites

Lorne Dufour

register sacred events:
miniscule man
riding giant horse
in the moonlight

Quiet snowy skid trail
near a mile around
north end of some
small frozen lake
deep in northern lands
where ancient magic
stillness
exists

My sweetheart lit
the lamp, set it
centre window
of the barn

Previous page: Dora was a gentle Belgian-Clydesdale cross.

*

How well he knew it, I wouldn't really appreciate 'til weeks later when I heard a great ruckus, hooting and hollering and the thundering of hooves all around my little cabin. I ran to the door and flung it open upon a scene right out of the nineteenth century. The men were driving all the wild horses right down the main street of the village, and between me and the church there came Irvin, the man with whom I had been talking about the dangers of motorcycles. He was mounted on a beautiful black cayuse. He swung right by my porch and waved his hat at me. He was smiling and I could feel the pride of the man like a rush of solar wind as he rode past. I never heard anyone mention motorbikes around there again.

Standing on the porch as the dust of the galloping horses settled on my shoulders and the cries of the proud horsemen faded in the distance, I realized one thing for sure: no matter how much things are changing, how much "progress" is taking place, these people will never lose their connection to the horse: never. I'll bet money on that.

Lorne Dufour

Mirror Full of Horses

One horse cantering
out of the mirror
taking my life
with him, my perceptional
power no longer reflective
not on the surface of still lakes
not on the surface of great poems
totally freed by perception
by a horse, my teacher
out of my mirror

Etiquette

There were very few days when one of my twenty-four students did not manage to put an arm around my neck at least once during the day. It was the children who made me aware of the true gentleness of the Shuswap people. John and I were working long days to create a terrific amount of individual programming. Our plan was that within a year or two, after successfully reopening a school that had been closed for eight years, we would have each of our students up to the grade level appropriate for their age. We had adequate help to get the job done too: most of it came from our students and their exceptional understanding of true etiquette, a kind that would make Emily Post think twice.

For example, one day at school I must have appeared preoccupied and perhaps even a little grumpy, because just around recess time, when the children had tolerated me for a quarter of the day, Kelly, the kid with that glint of mischief in his eyes, came up to me, placed his hand on my shoulder, and said: "Lorne, dit you get up on the wrong side of the bett today?"

Sxoxomic School (Alkali Lake Reserve), 2009.
Photo Vici Johnstone.

I realized then that the children were not enjoying my company and that I had better try to catch up with them immediately. His question changed my entire mood that day, and I was very thankful and humbled.

Lorne Dufour

I had developed the habit of bringing a box of oranges and a box of apples, whenever they were available at the grocery stores in Williams Lake, and placing them at the entrance to our class. In a few days they would all disappear. I would tell students that if they felt like enjoying some vitamin C fruit they could just help themselves. They did so quietly. No one asked me for an apple. It wasn't necessary. Many times the students would visit in the evenings, too, in the little log cabin behind the church. A lady friend, Pirjo from Williams Lake, had made me a beautiful wizard cape, all sparkled up in silver stars and a new moon. She made me a tall, pointed cap as well. It was the headgear one might expect upon an ancient astronomer. Equipped with my costume and a pair of binoculars, I began hosting Astronomy Night at my cabin once a week. Astronomy Night was for my class and anyone else who wished to attend. Each Wednesday, when the weather allowed, my little cabin would slowly fill up with eager astronomers and I would focus on some special star or constellation, making sure the students could pick it out of the star patterns. Perhaps I would tell them a story about one of the stars or constellations. Occasionally one of the students would open my refrigerator. Invariably, I would hear someone say: "Lorne, I will have a piece of watermelon." It was more a statement of fact than a request.

"Of course, go ahead," I would respond.

Sometimes someone else would say: "I will take one, too, Lorne."

There was such honest truthfulness about the children, it was always a privilege to share my fridge with them. While I lived in the priest's cabin, I never once locked the door if I left for the weekend, and never once did anyone ever go into the cabin when I was away. Deep in their hearts, the children were instilled with respect.

The Invisible One

I had a pair of cross-country skis. When winter arrived, with its big blanket of snow over the street, I would don my european knickers, those long woollen stockings, and I would ski to school. The students always greeted me with smiles. One time, one of the ladies, one of the parents, told me that the parents called me Mister Dressup, which I really enjoyed.

Usually when one of the parents visited me I would make them a cup of tea and we would talk about the progress of their child in class or whatever the parent wished to discuss. One day a man dropped by, a man I had never seen all year. He seemed to know I was not a priest but a school teacher, yet he had come to visit with me. After I made him a cup of tea

The cabin that Lorne lived in at Alkali Lake was originally the Priest's cabin.

he asked if I was enjoying living there and teaching. We made small talk for a while and later he left.

Shortly afterwards, one of the ladies came to visit me.

"I saw a person came to visit you today."

"Yes. Did you see him? Who is that fellow? He never left his name or told me anything about himself. Does he live out in the meadows or on another reserve?"

She did not tell me his name or where he lived or anything, so I began to realize that something about his visit bothered her. Looking quietly and firmly into my eyes she said, "Should he return, don't visit with him again."

"Why not? Why shouldn't I offer him tea or anything?"

"He has become someone we no longer 'see.'" She told me. "He is not someone we 'see.' Now that you are one of us too, he is now someone you no longer 'see.'"

She would not tell me why we could no longer "see" this person, but I knew she was serious.

Later on someone told me that this man's wife and children had died in a house fire when he had become totally inebriated. He was not taken to the white police, but he *had* become invisible to everyone on the reserve. Fortunately, he never returned to my little cabin.

Opposite: Celina earned a degree at UBC and returned to Alkali Lake where she taught the children for another twenty-five years.

Celina's Drum

Celina was one of the elders who came to the school two or three times a week to teach the Shuswap language. She would gather the kids into a large room we had in the basement. John, who had taken a scholarly interest in the roots and development of the language, had set up the lessons for her. The children enjoyed the courses and were progressing well. In most of the homes there was a lot of support for the language, too, but in some English had all but replaced their native tongue. The band as a whole was concerned, and hoped that the language courses would reverse the trend. For John and I, we not only respected the people for wanting to retain their language, we really encouraged them in every way we could to save it from extinction. Still, in our more cynical moments

Lorne Dufour

we couldn't help thinking that if you really want somebody to learn something you should not teach it at school. Think about it: what do *you* remember about the Riel rebellion? And you studied that in school! Of course, to think like that in our setting was almost treasonable. Besides, the natives themselves would teach the course. That alone, we hoped, would nullify the effects of public education.

I remember very well one particular day when Celina arrived with a drum. She was listing into the wind when she arrived and drew our attention because it wasn't the day for the language lessons.

"You going to teach Shuswap today?"

The kids enjoyed the classroom time, but history paled next to Celina's drumming and singing. L-R: Robert Chelsea, John Johnson, Jimmy Paul, Carlo Ignatius, Kelly Johnson, Willy Johnson and Ralph Johnson.

"Yeah, gonna teach them kits history lesson." She smiled at me.

"Well, I will send the kids down to you in the basement in a few minutes if that would be OK?"

"Goot Lorne, you dew that."

"OK Celina."

The kids drifted down to where Celina was set up, and pretty soon my class was empty and the unmistakable sound of native chanting came seeping up through the floorboards. How I wished I had been born Shuswap that day! Celina was singing a song in Shuswap. A sad song. It had to be a sad story she was telling. Those words were so full of weeping. Soon all the children were singing with her. It was a song as old as the rings in the pine. The kids gave themselves up to it entirely and they sang until their individual personalities merged into a long continuous wailing chant. The song sounded like it was filled with the pain of living, the pain of birth and the pain of loss. If a person were to break it down somehow into actual words and names and histories, the way other cultures record history, the songs would reveal everything from the joy of childbirth to the deep despair of the drunken suicide. The communication in the songs would become so compressed and intensified by the magnitude of human living and human misery that no one person could sustain the song alone, and no one person could possibly receive all of its power. The song that Celina and the children were singing was a prayer to the Creator. When they were finished, I knew the class would not be ready to study spelling and reading, so we went down to the creek, where the boys netted some small trout.

It was that day that Eddy asked me an interesting question.

"Hey, Lorne?"

It was a fine spring day and dust was rising in little minia-
ture clouds around our feet as we walked back to school.

"Yes, Eddy?"

"Dit you ever see any reel Indians?"

"Real Indians???"

"Yeah, you know."

"You mean with feathers and war paint and everything?"

"Yeah, reel Indians."

Eddy was a very special person. I knew he would grow and
he would understand throughout the lived experiences of his
own life, that while nationalities are important, finding your-
self, the real person that others love, well, that is even more
important. Many years after this conversation with Eddy, an
old friend wrote me a letter. He had returned to the States and
he was filling me in on his children. At the time his daugh-
ter, Rachel, was in the second grade. He picked the kids up
from school the day Elvis died. Her teacher was crying and
all the girls were crying. Rachel, that evening, lay in bed and
cried. The next morning, a Saturday, while eating her pancakes
Rachel asked, "Daddy, who was Elvis Presley anyway?"

Now, for me it was interesting to hear little Eddy ask the
big question about Indians. It came from the poverty and mis-
ery of his background, but I knew Eddy: even as he asked that
question he was beginning to figure things out for himself. I
realized that he would be taking great pride in the discovery
that "real" Indians will always be larger than any stereotype. A
"real" Indian would be as large as Eddy himself.

The Owl

I saw you
in the woods today
diving into a brush pile

then standing there
your back to me
motionless

a tiny monk
at silent
prayer

suddenly lifting
a miniscule mole
clutched in death

its tail
trailing
in the wind

Lorne Dufour

The Owl's Call

Halloween rolled around and we divvied up our work. John was going to organize the hotdogs and hot chocolate and Ron was going to make sure everyone had a ride down to the lake for the fireworks. My job included taking a group of kids and building a big bonfire down there. The fireworks were set for around nine that night. My crew and I arrived at the lake around six-thirty to begin gathering wood for the party. We built her tall and wide and she would burn like a giant torch in the darkness of that terrible Halloween night. We had gathered most of the logs we needed when I first noticed the owl. It was a sound at first, a sound that originated somewhere off in the dusk and came to us quite clearly as we worked on the fire. It was moving closer to us, and as we were finishing I was sure that the owl was within fifty feet of us. None of the students had mentioned it, but I noticed that my group had become very quiet, as if something they did not like was happening. They had become quiet and serious.

I turned to Ralph, who was one of the boys with me, and I asked him: "Hear the owl?"

He held my gaze for a moment before answering, then looking away he simply said, "It's John." Then he looked directly into my eyes. The way the others were watching us I knew Ralph was resolute.

"What do you mean, 'It's John?' That is an owl!"

"No, Lorne. It's John," came the serious reply. The group shifted around nervously, almost embarrassed that I didn't know my friend's voice.

The entire affair frightened me, so I said, "Look, you guys, let's jump in the truck and drive up the road. I bet a million bucks we're gonna flush an owl out of one of these trees."

Always willing to go for a ride the group climbed into the truck. I turned the truck and headed up in direction of the ominous "Hooo Hooo Hooo HOOOOO," but the night there had become as quiet as velvet drapes in the wind. We drove to the end of the lake, turned around and headed back. Just as we reached the area of our prepared bonfire, a large, grey owl dropped off of a limb with wide, silent strokes, flew directly across the road in front of us to disappear in the darkness on the other side. Seeing it was a kind of victory for me, I excitedly turned to the children and said: "See! There is your owl, kids!"

The boy nearest me looked at me the way an adult will sometimes indulge a contradictory child and he said with infinite, sad, patience: "It's John."

I could see that the conversation was closed. They knew something, they had told me what they knew, and I was acting like a fool belabouring the subject. I said no more, and we drove back up to the village in silence. They obviously were not about to explain their knowledge. I left the group, which split up and headed home in various directions throughout the reserve.

When I reached the teacherage, John was sitting at the kitchen table drinking a cup of coffee. That place had a meager layer of linoleum stretched over a concrete floor and that night it felt like a cold house. I studied my friend and he must have seen the concern in my eyes. I didn't really know how to tell him about the owl.

Lorne Dufour

Invisible Geese

This morning a great flock
of geese filled
the sky with their
lonely calls

It took a long time
'til their cries dwindled
down into a memory

So vast were their numbers
they had come from
the stars in the palms
of my hands

I waved in the direction
their dreams were heading
a scattering of ancestors
waved back at me

And in no place
could they be seen

Previous page: Eileen Harry and Doreen Johnson, 1975.

*

"What is it Lorne?"

"Oh, nothing really…"

"What's the matter, Lorne? Everything OK with the fire?" God, but that teacherage was a cold, sobering place, complete as it was with bare cupboards, a large sink to wash dishes in, and that slate-like floor. I will never forget the sight of John sitting at the table that night. He looked so lonely in that place, even though everyone loved him.

"Yeah, it ain't that, John. It's something else, something… well…."

"Well what?"

"Well, we were fixing the fire, you know, and there was this big owl in a tree, sort of hooting at us, and it was kind of spooky."

"Yeah????"

"Thing is, that when the kids heard it they said it was you, John. They said it was you, even after I flushed it out of the bushes down there and they seen it flying across the road. They still said it was you, John." John just looked at me for a moment. He didn't say anything. It made me uncomfortable, so I added: "Hell, I don't know, John, but somehow and for some reason that they did not wish to talk about, that is what they said."

I walked over to the cupboard, chose a mug and carried it to the stove and poured myself a cup of coffee. After that, John and I talked over the plans for the evening. Everything was ready to go and everyone seemed pretty happy to be going and enjoying fireworks. It would be a real good time, hooting owl or not. It would be a good evening.

The Team

John and I worked sixteen hours every day getting the school on its feet, getting the different reading programs sorted out, placing the children in the exact, right learning situation unique for each of them. I wanted so much to be successful that I put all pride aside and didn't hesitate to go to more experienced teachers and ask for help when I needed it. We did receive help from the school district in Williams Lake: Martin

Jacob Roper with Lorne, Deno Chelsea, Douglas Robbins, Henry Johnson and Alfred Harry.

Hamm, for one, helped and let us know how much we needed the help, but we accepted all of it and kept going ahead. I had been looking for John for a long time. He was such a beautiful person, I would gladly risk my life for him, let alone work around the clock with him. It all came down to the night of the bonfire, when so many issues were clarified in its light. Now thirty years later I can begin to see them for what they were.

When I went to Alkali I had been living the gypsy life for nearly eighteen years. In many ways I felt that I had found a home. It was too much to expect or to ask, of course, and I didn't realize that I had been asking for a home until later, when I was not invited to teach there again and suddenly there was no home there for a wandering gypsy. The truth is that the band was having great difficulties just surviving and the year we were there was the first year in many that someone had not been killed in a fight or something like that. Phyllis and Andy, the leaders at that time, were making great advances in their battle against alcohol, and while they did love and shelter me for a while they just couldn't be my family, and it was unfair of me to hope that they could. The home of a true gypsy is his heart anyway, and though I not only knew that and had been living gypsy-style for so many years, still, way down deep I yearned for a place. I went there looking for it, I suppose, and learned, finally, truthfully and without question, that my home is and was where it always was and will be, that is wherever I happen to be and within the circle of love and strength that I can generate and share. The night of the bonfire, my love for John was tested by powers great enough to stir up the wind to hurricane proportions and turn a tiny lake into a raging miniature ocean in seconds.

Lorne Dufour

Wind

Fragments of cedar confetti
onto the tent
patterning pagodas across
the canvas

Shotgun explosions
puff ball into sound
drifting across the slope
celebrating the season
and the stew pot

The wind comes
snapping timbers
sky pillars booming
roaring through the pines
wild music cleaning and scouring

shuffling rubbing the mountain
with its wild curry comb

Hundred-foot fir trees
bear dance, swing sixty feet
from side to side and all of
the mountain is green and
yellow stormy ocean

Down here
on the floor of the sea
we little fishes, squirrel,
horse, rabbit, bear, bird and
people dart about
eyes quick
hearts   quick

Opposite: Alkali Lake. Photo Vici Johnstone.

Lorne Dufour

The Overturned Boat

The fireworks were to be lit from a small rowboat out on the lake. It was equipped with an anchor on a long chain, a small outboard engine and a large piece of plywood. Martin had secured the plywood upright, midship. He had holes in it for his hands. This design allowed him to place rockets on a launching pad and safely ignite them, and then use the plywood as a shield when the fireworks burst for the stars. When that devil wind came howling down the valley, he was anchored about eighty yards from shore on the shallow little lake. The wind caught the plywood shield and flipped the boat like a cat flipping a chip of wood. Someone hollered: "The boat turned over! Martin's in the water! Martin's in the water!"

Andy told someone to drive a truck down past the bonfire so we could set the headlights on the boat. We could see Martin then. He was sitting on the transom of the boat, whose floating surface had suddenly become very small. Martin was waving his arms and shouting, "Help! Help! Help!"

Shouting for help is rarely a good way to save your life. Usually a person can survive without help, although there are times when without outside help we can lose our lives and our souls. Eighty yards or so. I thought Martin should swim for shore, and I figured a person could make it one way without difficulty. I knew I could make it. Martin was thirty-nine years old, in perfect physical condition and very strong, but he was terrified. Earlier that very evening he had confided to his wife that he had a dismal feeling that should his boat go down he would not survive. He had suffered a premonition and that alone almost paralyzed him. At the time of his conversation with his wife, the little lake was calm and there was no reason to expect a wind that would arrive like a dark curse and flip his boat over. The wind did come though, and Martin slowly filled up with absolute terror. His fear of death took over his mind.

Ron and Andy jumped into Andy's pickup and went rushing off to find a boat, while a group of us men lined the shore, watching Martin in the lights of the truck and discussing the situation. Steve Belleau wanted to swim out to help him, but I discouraged him from attempting to do that. My reasoning was that since the water was close to freezing a person would be risking hypothermia by exposing himself to its grip for the time required to swim both ways, while Martin could easily make it to shore in ten to fifteen minutes, max.

Ron and Andy returned with the bad news that there were no other boats closer than fifteen or twenty miles distance, and they left for another search. Meanwhile, one of Martin's sisters waded out into the freezing lake, almost up to her hips. She held a fence rail in her hands and made quite a picture placing herself so helplessly between the group on shore and her stricken brother on the overturned boat. She gestured to us on shore, as if someone should swim out and bring him in with the fence rail. She was a healthy-looking woman, with a good layer of fat shielding her from total penetration by the freezing water, and I thought that she would have a better chance of swimming both ways than any of our group would. It also occurred to me that she recognized the danger of attempting to swim that far, but she didn't mind sacrificing one of us in the attempt.

John arrived precisely when she climbed out of the lake. I don't know where he had been up 'til then, but when I saw him standing at the edge of the lake, and he had already peeled his jeans off and was pulling his shirt over his head, I knew John so well that I knew I could never talk him out of going in and saving Martin. John assumed the position of total responsibility for everything. That's just the way John was.

I also knew that I would have to go with him to make sure they got to shore all right.

I walked over to him and said, "I guess you have decided to swim for him, hey John?"

"Yes, I'm going to go get him."

"OK, then I will come and help you, but put your jeans back on and leave your socks and your shirt on."

I figured we would need the insulation that clothing could provide.

"I will come, but we better take that fence rail and each take an end. We can put Martin in the middle of the rail. Coming back, we can pull for shore together."

It was a good plan. Teamwork was really required. A good plan, but a dangerous one: dangerous for me and John. It could have worked. Team work, dog shit!

That Cold Memory
(1995)

Somewhere between mountains
mountains of snow
and some other mountain
where only dreamers go
Bill arrived
dressed like an Arizona biker
boots jeans and leather jacket
while with the mercy of wolves
winter crunched down on us
greeting him with fifty-six below

Tent walls frosted up
yet warm enough near the stove
Bill volunteering to feed the fire
without even being asked
The memory of that cold is fading
yet we will always remember
Mom and I and the children
how much we enjoyed the rest

The Swim

We waded out chest deep and pushed off. The wind was breaking off the tops of the wave peaks. As it howled across the surface it created a sheet of spray over our heads. We were entirely encapsulated in water, and as we made our way towards the boat and Martin our bodies began to feel the effects of the cold. Our joints were freezing up on us. I noticed that my wrists, my knees and my ankles were beginning to grow numb. The cold sank into our bodies, causing us to sink deeper into the water, so that when we were within shouting distance of the boat only a small part of our heads and some of our faces were above water, which was covered for the most part by the sheets of spray covering the lake. I knew that by the time we reached the boat we were in serious trouble and would need every resource we had to get back to shore.

When Martin saw us struggling towards him he shouted into the wind. "What do we have here?"

That seemed to me to be a little bizarre, a little imperious, as if the man was holding court and was being presented with petitioners or something.

John shouted back. "The teachers. It's the teachers." We kept pulling closer and closer to the overturned craft.

Martin shouted: "Who is it?"

"The teachers from the school," John shouted back.

After a moment, likely seconds but it seemed like minutes to me: "Oh, the teachers." There was a pause then. Following it Martin asked, "Well what do you propose?" My God. What do you propose???

"Martin" I shouted, causing him to look directly at me, since I was closest to the boat. "Help us out of the water."

He reached down for me and lifted me up and out of the water in one easy motion with one hand. His strength was phenomenal and I thought that he was pumping pure adrenaline and was possibly in a state of partial shock. I pulled myself up beside him, then hauled John up beside me, so that we sat three abreast on the transom of the boat. John was having difficulty regaining his breath. His breathing was shallow and fast, too shallow and much too fast. I realized that we needed to have full control of our breathing in order to have the strength for the long pull to shore.

"John" I said. "Try to slow down your breathing and breath slowly and deeply."

"I'm OK."

His breath came in pants, dog-like.

"No, you are not OK, John. You are nearly frozen. You need to get your breath back. You need to slow your heart down."

We sat that way for a few minutes, maybe it was five minutes, while John, with his thin arms hugging himself, attempted to get control of his breathing. I had already done so—the boxing training much earlier in my life and the two years I had spent studying Hatha Yoga, had made me very much aware of the fact that we needed steady breathing to sustain a forced swim or any kind of vigorous activity, especially in adverse conditions.

"Fill the bottom of your lungs John, then the middle, then the top of your lungs."

John was slowly beginning to breathe more naturally and I was rubbing his back so he would begin to feel his body again.

Martin asked me: "What do you teachers propose?"

"We had originally planned to swim back together, but maybe we should just stay on the boat till it blows to shore, it's pretty near freezing in that water, Martin."

"The boat is anchored. It is impossible to free the anchor without diving beneath the boat. Even then we couldn't free it."

None of us had the slightest desire to submerge ourselves in those conditions; our swim had illustrated only too clearly that it was difficult to maintain any kind of buoyancy at all.

"That's out then," I agreed. "So we propose to swim back together. Martin, you have a life ring. That's great. You can ride in the centre of the fence rail. John and I will take the front and back. John and I can pull for shore and you can help by swimming and by maintaining the pole above your life ring. Then we can rest if necessary. Sinking was a real problem coming out."

"Maybe they will bring another boat."

"No, not right now, Martin. They couldn't find one here. That's why John and I came out. We figured you couldn't stand the cold out here for too long and they may not return with another boat for half an hour or so."

I noticed that John's breathing was a little closer to normal by this time, but that he still didn't have the energy for talking. I knew he was in bad shape and figured that we should head back soon before the freezing spray and wind chilled us beyond the ability to move.

Meanwhile Martin had come to a decision, a decision which would cost him and John their lives. "I think it best that we strike off on our own."

"You mean each man for himself, Martin?" I was stunned by his pronouncement.

"Yes, I think we would have a better chance that way."

I didn't argue with him. I figured I could get John to shore safely and if Martin wished to swim for it there was no reason to think he wouldn't make it. It was strange, though. We had risked our lives to come and help him, only to discover that he could help us, all of us, should he agree to work with us, but he thought helping us would cause him too much difficulty. He had heavy clothing and a life ring, so he was insulated and buoyant. The wind would likely blow him down course, but by tracking towards our bonfire and the truck lights he could hit shore within a few minutes. I told him that.

"OK, Martin, just head for those lights. There are people all along the shore line. As soon as you touch bottom, someone will help you out of the lake. Just head for the fire and the truck and don't stop 'til you touch bottom."

He left us then, without another word, and began swimming towards shore. He was making steady progress and had gone a good sixty feet before I turned back to John.

"You OK now, John?"

"I'm OK, I'm OK, g-g-got my b-b-breath now."

"John, you are not okay. We could drown here. We got to put everything we have into this swim, John. Everything."

"Y-y-yes."

He was shivering almost uncontrollably. Although my wrists and ankles and knees felt slightly numb, I was in a much stronger condition.

"Look, John. We count our strokes, OK?" He nodded.

"Take maybe three hundred strokes to get to shore, maybe four hundred. Don't stop counting. Keep your concentration and stay focused. You got it?"

Again John just nodded, but he looked calmer and more in control now. "Don't waste your strength hollering for help, John. Just don't let go of the fence rail, and keep pulling. We got to make it."

"Yeah, let's go."

Before re-entering the water I checked on Martin's progress.

He had covered another thirty or forty feet and was about a hundred feet closer to shore. He was in trouble, though. I could see that because he was bringing his arms straight up from his sides and pounding them down on the water like a baby bird attempting to fly for the first time.

"Swim, Martin! Swim!" I yelled into the wind, but I doubt that he could hear me from that distance and in that wind.

"Well, Martin is on his own now," I thought, as we slipped off of the boat and re-entered the water, which didn't seem so cold this time. It probably didn't feel as cold as it had formerly because our bodies were already beginning to freeze.

There was nothing more we could do for Martin. I hoped that even though he was swimming poorly he might make enough progress to reach shore. He had been calm and clear when he was on the boat, but obviously terrified. He knew his life was in danger. I hoped that fear would keep him pumping for shore. As for his decision to go it alone, that was something we had to accept. When you find yourself in a dangerous situation with two other people, with one mistake you may never see the sun rise again; you may never see your wife and family again; you may never even see a pile of dog shit again. A man has to consider all this. He considers everything. He decides what is best and Martin decided it was best to head to shore without John and me. Perhaps he thought we would slow him down if he had to hold the middle of the fence rail. Perhaps he thought that he would slow us down. I never really knew his reasons, but when all the chips are on the table and somebody makes his play, you have no choice but to go along with it. I had hoped he would return with us. I figured three men swimming together, shouting encouragement, keeping one another afloat, well we would make it, and having thought it over thousands of times since I know I was right.

Covering the Barn
(the neighbours 2003)

We had provided logs
built a great three-dimensioned building
complete with calf areas and a run off
for loading cows and calves
a hundred and twenty feet by
forty feet

That is large
and so permanent we put a tarp
over it like a circus tent
we hooked it up to the clouds
and made it into a dream place

Someone said should the wind arrive
in full force it will tear the roof
off the barn but Danny and I knew different

We understood something larger than success
larger than permanence larger than pride
we knew that should the wind arrive
we would all stay inside the barn
and all of us would float off
into the clouds forever
let the wind come home
let the wind come home

We eased into the water, John first, taking the end of the fence rail with him. I came off the boat with the rail in my right hand. This was a small mistake, definitely not desirable because the main power of my body is my right arm. Infantile paralysis had struck me as a child and my left shoulder muscles had atrophied, leaving the arm useless for certain activities. Having used the right arm to compensate I had built it up until it was much more powerful than a normal arm would have been and this was the arm I wanted to use to swim with. The left would be more than adequate for holding onto the rail. I dipped under the rail, intending to duck-dive and surface on the other side. In those conditions this was a mistake, a near fatal mistake that really frightened me. I should have simply lifted the rail over my head, because when I went under, the cold power of the lake sucked me under a good three or four feet. I came up sputtering and choking, having swallowed a mouthful of Alkali Lake.

For a second I was disoriented, then I heard John shouting my name: "Lorne! Lorne! Here! Over here!" I saw him immediately and reached out for my end of the rail. I pulled it in under my left arm.

"OK, John," I shouted back to him, back those twelve or fourteen feet between us, back along a cedar fence rail that held us together. I shouted to John: "Let's go!" I took a bearing over my shoulder on the truck lights and the bonfire and began counting, deep, powerful back strokes for shore. Although John was, as I said, no more than fourteen feet from me, I couldn't see him without stopping and treading water, but I could feel his weight at the end of the rail. After twenty strokes or so I cast a glance over my shoulder and was relieved to see that we were right on course. With renewed vigor I began pulling my body through the water and maintained my count. I believe I had counted more than two hundred strokes before I began to lose it. At that time we had been exposed to near freezing water and a cold, numbing wind for over half an hour. I could no longer feel my joints at all. Every point of articulation in my body had long since lost sensation and I had slowly lost my awareness of even this fact of my condition. Hypothermia was setting in. I no longer remembered that I was clutching the fence rail. In fact, I was beginning to wonder where the hand was coming from, the hand that kept surfacing near my chest to describe an arc and to disappear above my head. It was as automatic as the hands of a watch and it fascinated me. I glanced towards the lights of the truck and was momentarily dazzled by their tremendous power and beauty. At the centre of the light was a core of white, yellow heat. Radiating out from that centre was a kaleidoscope of rainbow-coloured light. The force of it was hypnotic. Every infinite particle of light emanating from that source was perceptible to me, and I had to tear my eyes away from the beautiful sight. As my hand came out of the water again, tiny drops of water were filling with multicoloured light, and as they fell beside my face they exploded into amazingly powerful patterns of colour, and the hand kept describing that persistent arc.

It was as if my right arm had taken upon itself a mission, a mission to make it to shore with my body and with John's body. While this was happening, my body and my mind had somehow lost the desire to go anywhere. There was no longer any urgency to make it to shore, no fear of drowning in the lake, no discomfort whatsoever, just a feeling of being a special sort of spectator enjoying the wonderful details of perception.

Suddenly, coming through this visionary type of awareness came the whisper of a human voice. How strange and how startling. Why would anyone whisper to me when the wind was howling like a hurricane and it was impossible to hear beyond three or four feet? What were they saying?

"Help, help." Oh, someone is whispering for help. Who could be doing that?

Slowly my mind struggled up out of its dreamy technicolored world and I realized with a jolt that likely saved my life that it must be John who was calling for help. At first my reaction was to think that he must surely be in trouble, because we had discussed our swim and agreed not to waste our energy yelling while we pulled for shore. I stopped swimming then and looked to the end of the rail, which was still tightly clutched under my left arm. John likely thought we were not going to make it and was calling someone on shore to come out and help us. John was not at the end of the rail, though. He must have let it go. I cast about looking for him, but I could not see very far at the water level. I could see up on the bank where the truck and fire were above the level of the lake, but right at the level where we swam a person couldn't see more than ten feet, at best. Then something very strange happened: I rose above the lake to a level of about fifteen feet and looked around. I looked towards the last direction that I had located John's voice and I saw him throw up his arm and yell, "Help." With his arm directly over his head he disappeared under the water and didn't resurface. He was approximately sixty to eighty feet from where I was swimming.

Later, I learned that the people on shore had been watching us proceed towards them. We were doing fine and they were not concerned that we wouldn't make it, when all of a sudden John abandoned his end of the fence rail and started swimming with both arms at a right angle to the course we had taken. He swam parallel to shore not much more than fifty feet out. Then he stopped and began calling for help. He called two or three times, I was told, then disappeared before anyone on shore could swim out to help him. It happened very fast. I knew where he had gone down but I did not have the strength to swim there and dive for him. The wind was still howling, the water freezing and someone swam up behind me and whispered into my ear: "Do you need help, Lorne?"

God almighty, I thought, why must everyone whisper in a hurricane? For some perverse reason I deliberately whispered my response: "Yes, I could use some help."

Suddenly I felt something being pushed under my left arm. I pushed down to test its buoyancy to find that it could support my weight. I knew then that I had been saved. I also knew without a doubt that my friend John was gone.

Two figures appeared beside me in the water. One of them was Irvin, a big strong man and swimmer: "Where is John?"

"Out that way but he is gone. Don't go there, don't drown too," I said to him.

I was terrified that someone else might lose their life in that terrible little lake that night. Irvin swam towards the area where John had sunk from sight, but he returned alone.

Lorne Dufour

The Bonfire

Little did I know when the kids and I built that big bonfire that it would be one of the beacons that John and I would head for that night. Now as Steve helped me out of the water, having swum out with a cedar log to help me make the last thirty or forty feet, it was instrumental in saving my life. Somebody said: "Go ahead, stand by the fire, Lorne."

I stumbled over to the big fire, which had burned down some. I stood before it for a moment, then toppled headlong right into it. My legs simply folded and I had no control over my arms or legs at all. Jacob ran over and pulled me out of the fire and brushed the sparks off of me.

"Better get Lorne home quick," he shouted and carried me like a baby up to his truck. He set me on the seat, and his lady Angela climbed in on the other side of me.

"Better roll down the window," she said, and Jacob replied in an impatient voice,

"Good God, woman, Lorne is freezing. Don't roll the window down!"

This domestic interchange seemed somehow very humorous to me, but I could not even smile. The only place I had any feeling in my body whatsoever was down in the pit of my stomach. A little bonfire burned in my guts, just like the one the kids had helped me build on shore. It felt more like a flickering candle than a bonfire, but at least it was some actual sensation. I still did not feel sure that I would live. I could not even bring myself to talk, and I was growing very drowsy.

Had anyone else, anyone other than Jacob, taken me home, I may not have survived that evening. When finally I began to experience sensations along my back, where Jacob was pouring hot water, I knew that he and Steve had saved my life. It was big Jacob, making his prayer to God for his beautiful daughter, Rose Marie, who had died of hypothermia. Big Jacob, my good friend.

"You going to be alright now, Lorne." Jacob said.

"Yes, I'm OK now, Jacob. I'm getting my feelings back now. Feel my hands now."

He kept pouring pail after pail of very hot water down my spine, and while I felt totally exhausted, my ankles and my wrists and knees regained full sensitivity.

Lorne Dufour

Martin's Heart

Martin was not so lucky. I'd been right when I'd seen him from the transom of the boat: he had actually stopped swimming properly and had started banging his arms straight down beside him as he sat, with the life ring, almost perfectly straight up in the water. The wind began to draw him back out into the lake and before Ron returned with a boat, a boat he and Andy finally located twenty miles away from Alkali Lake, poor Martin the baron, he had beat his way into the heart of the darkness.

The wind was still ferocious when Ron returned. The rowboat was quite small, maybe twelve feet long, max. Ron pushed it out and rowed himself as quickly as possible in the direction the wind must have taken Martin. He was already two thirds of the way across the lake, floating: his head was not in the water, but he was no longer swimming, just floating because of his life ring. Ron yelled at him, and Martin turned and tried to respond. He was too weak to climb into the boat, and Ron knew he might overturn should he attempt to pull him in over the side. He pulled him over the stern far enough for Martin to hook his elbows over the backboard. Ron told me he kept shouting at Martin just to keep him awake. He told me he could see that by the time he found Martin the cold had seeped into his body. It didn't matter that he had long johns on and a vest and a life ring; he had been soaking in the cold water for almost an hour and he was losing the battle for his own life. Ron said he even swore at Martin a few times, anything he could think of to make Martin answer, but he received no response.

When Ron hit the nearest shore, some of the fellows were waiting for him. Martin was not communicating. They pulled

Martin out of the water and put him into a truck and drove immediately up to the ranch, where Martin's wife and sister were waiting for him. Still he was not communicating. They set him up beside the fireplace. It was the warmest place they could think of. Someone wrapped a big woollen blanket around him and his wife phoned the doctor. The doctor told them to keep Martin as warm as possible and he would be there as quickly as possible. If my friend, big Jacob, had taken Martin home he would have torn off his clothes like he did mine, he would have immediately put him in a bathtub, and he would have poured pail after pail of extremely hot water down his central nervous system, his spinal cord really, and he would have drawn the freezing cold out of his body. When someone wrapped Martin in a big blanket, they didn't take Martin's freezing clothes off of him. He was close to the fireplace, but the warm blanket around him just drove the cold into his heart, and before the doctor managed to arrive at Alkali Martin's heart had stopped.

Reflection

Coming onto the lake
in late afternoon light
the reflection is perfect
no ripples, no exaggeration
everything perfectly cloned
by our power to perceive
our natural desire
to understand

Has it come from childhood
when once we saw the perfect lake
and the reflection reminds us
takes us back to perfection
when only love filled our atoms
does the perfect reflection
repeat the notion of our destiny
that life is the dream and beyond
is the reality

All water
coming down from the mountains
and the mountains celebrated
in the picture nature creates
the fish floating in the air
the spirits swimming
in the depth of the lake

Funerals

My beloved friend John Rathjen had drowned. Some of the guys found his body the next morning. There was no wind then, and it didn't take them too long because some of them had seen him throw up his arm and sink. My friend throwing his arm up and calling for help and I couldn't help him. My friend that woke me up by whispering "help" in my freezing ears. My friend that did so much to reopen the school at Alkali, to help the people prepare themselves to run their own school. My friend that helped them set up a language course for their own language. My friend John who helped reawaken Indian pride.

There was a big funeral for Martin. He was buried on the ranch. Almost the entire reserve attended his funeral. They came and they sang for him and his family. I never attended, as I had gone to Rathjen's family in the Okanagan. As John had cautioned me, they were a very religious family. In fact, his father was some kind of evangelical minister. A few years later, I sent his mother a copy of my book of poems, *Spit on Wishes*. She told me she liked it very much, but way down deep I figured she didn't like the swear word in it. I had written about life in general and sometimes when you do that a four letter word rises to the surface of poetry. It did in my book and I bet she didn't like it. When I went to the funeral there in Kelowna, it was very difficult to look upon John in a casket. A few years later John's father died, so when I sent my book to John's mom, well his sister, his mom and I were the only family left.

Lorne Dufour

The Bridge
(1982)

It was the black vest
I figured and white shirt
western-style caused
the Hutterite women
normally unapproachable
to smile at me
one time my sweetheart
teased me when they
in town one day
surrounded me, looking
for all the world, she
said, like a flock
of dowdy chickens with
a little rooster

Later though I thought
because she was so beautiful our children
so healthy, our horses
so fine, when we travelled
like gypsies trekkin de drom
through south Alberta
the Hutterites welcomed us
and our vardo, our summer
home on wheels

Once, as we approached
the Castle River
a family of Hutterites
crowded native-style

into a pickup stopped us
invited us to camp on
one of their fields
Don't turn off at the tourist
campsite they told us
you cross the bridge
over the Castle River
there is a gate
on your right near the river
that is Hutterite land
your horses can graze
in the field, you can
stay as long as you wish

We crossed the silver river
and they sheltered us
and remembered
their own history
their families
in horse-drawn
wagons

There was a glimmer of colours
fountains of wildflowers
green fields golden corn
and the magic river
but we remember
in vivid detail
those quiet and powerful
people who had dedicated
their lives living
in black and white

Lorne Dufour

Moving On

The year John left us, when he was only twenty-nine years old, we all shared our grief at Alkali Lake. Those good people made a great muskox circle around my pain and helped me to slowly get back on my feet. I played hockey with the second team, the Eagles, and we had fantastic and spirited games with the Renegades, their first team. The Renegades had a history involving many great players, truly great like Pat Chelsea, David Johnson and that Sylista, the player that Lester Patrick offered a contract with the New York Rangers. The Renegades took me on for a few great games and I played right wing that year. Sport and humour, two powerful methods to build inner strength and to hold a community together. One time, after a game in Williams Lake, we were driving a truckload of players, and I told the boys in the cab that we were driving past my sweetheart Diana's home in town. She was a librarian and some of my students and I would visit her weekly in order to increase our reading skills. I was falling in love with her. Sort of boasting as we drove past her little house in town I told the Renegade players that her cat had just had a litter of eight or nine kittens. Someone quickly reacted to that information, saying: "Lorne, is that a cat house?"

Of course this earned a good laugh. Strange, isn't it, how after so many years have passed, after you might have been involved in many serious, globe-worry type conversations with people, it is the little things that stick with you all your life! Little things that were set in a perfect synch with the birds and the bees.

A year or two after I left Alkali and headed into the forest with my lady and our horses, Alkali built a new school and Celina got her teaching certificate and began a permanent teaching position in the new school. Fred Johnson, our Renegade goalie and one of Alkali's gifted carvers, became principal of that school for years. One time when we met at a hockey game twenty or so years later, I asked Freddy how he was doing.

"I'm doing fine, Lorne, and you, how are things with you?"

"Everything is OK, Freddy, and, of course, we still have that beautiful carving you made for me and Diana." The carving is a family-theme totem pole, with a dad and a mom and two infants all scattered in pieces, live arms and feet and faces and breasts, all around the totem pole, very beautiful and a cherished piece of art in our home, be it a house like it is today or a tent or a wagon as it was for so many years.

"I am wondering about it though Freddy. When you made it you only put two babies on it, and since then we have had a third baby."

"Well, Lorne, you bring it back to me and I will figure out a way to put another baby on it."

"Are you doing much carving now, Freddy?"

"I no longer have time for carving, Lorne. The work I do now is too important. I no longer have time for artwork."

That was sad news in some ways, as Freddy is a true artist, and his power is reflected in everything he touches, be it chanting or drumming, carving or teaching. He plays a major role in the movie *Honor Of All,* which has rounded the globe as a true story designed to help anyone anywhere with an alcohol problem. Alkali, with its many new homes, its development of the Meadows, its new school and its courage to become one of the most important Indian reserves on this planet, is a place I am so proud to have known as my home.

Lorne Dufour

147

Lorne Dufour

The Wind Grew Strong

One Halloween long after the drowning, I backed my little pickup down a boat ramp so that with the back tires in the water and the emergency brake engaged I could easily fill the water barrel secured just inside the tailgate. I was camped within a mile of the lake, my horses were in a pole corral, and they needed water. As I stood on the back bumper and steadily dipped my bucket, the wind began to grow stronger and stronger, most likely the same wind that had torn itself into anger the time John and I tried to save Martin von Riedemann's life, until the waves began to beat against my legs and to lift the back tires so that the emergency brake no longer held me safely to the shore. It had become dark, and it took me a few seconds to hear John warning me that I was in danger. I finally realized that the truck was floating backwards into the lake.

I climbed into the back real quickly and then through the window into the driver's seat. I started the engine and attempted to drive out of the lake, yet I kept being drawn out further and further from shore. I climbed out the window again before the water began to enter the cab. I won't ever forget standing on the slanted roof of that little Dodge Ram 4 x 4. The headlights had tilted up towards the crowns of the spruce trees on the shore, the box had filled with water, and we were sinking. I had my caulk boots on and left deep scratches on the hood as I leapt as far as I could towards shore, thinking I would land in water not deeper than my waist. When I hit the water, though, I went deeper and deeper, until the lake sealed up over my head. I managed to pull myself out of the lake, and found myself in total darkness, as the truck had disappeared. It was just as cold and dark as that terrible night at Alkali. I knew hypothermia

‧would overtake me if I didn't get help as quickly as possible. Ah, sweet John, I ran a good mile to the nearest place where someone lived and beat on their door.

The next day, two old friends helped me pull the truck out of the lake. After a few attempts from a rowboat, we managed to hook a cable onto the bumper of the truck. Slowly, very slowly, we winched it onto the shore. I kept thinking about John, how they slowly brought his body out of Alkali Lake the morning after he had drowned.

I could not help but think that John had been with me that night when the truck went down.

Previous pages: L-R: Agnes Johnson, Diane Robbins, Gayle Belleau and Adam Dufour, 1975.

Experiencing Tereina Marie

Everything froze, minus
thirty-five for days
benumbing us and our horses
their steel shoes
proclaiming the Arctic

Today it warmed up
a heavenly plus six
Our daughter comes tumbling
out onto the cabin porch
wearing summer cutoffs

Tereina our Sun Dance
while age and wisdom
cling to the side effects
of cold winters
still she brings us
back to beginnings
and every moment of life
is a fortune.

WAIKTHA (Weytk)

I was Carlo's teacher
once many many years ago
my left arm rendered
increasingly weak
from infantile paralysis
just like my ancestor

his right hand bereft
of a thumb and two fingers
from a saw mill accident
near ten years past

Standing in the library
totally consumed
by a million books
I heard someone greet me
"Waiktha" the Shuswap way

Carlo and Robert
appearing as quiet as trees
among the endless voices
Carlo repeated "Waiktha
our teacher"
extending his left hand
and I responded with my right

After all these years
we both offered the best we had
it was more than enough
it was waiktha

Afterword

—Ivy Chelsea, 2009
Graduate Student, UNBC
First Nations Studies

The death that hit home to me was the death of my Grade 6 teacher, John Rathjen, on October 31, 1975. There were fifteen of us in his class and I hope that one day we can come together and write a memoir for John.

The previous year was a transitional period for Alkali Lake. With help from Alan Haig-Brown, the First Nations Education Coordinator for the Cariboo-Chilcotin School District, the Alkali Lake chief and council had just taken over education transfer dollars. For the first time the band could hire their own teachers. That is how we met three new teachers: John Rathjen, Lorne Dufour, and Ron Fern. Lorne taught the younger class, while John taught us, the older teenage students. The way Alan and dad share this history is that "it was the first time that cowboys had to work with hippies."

I had not been sure if I would like any of the new teachers, because the DIA (Department of Indian Affairs) teachers that had been working with us had been just ornery and mean. So, as John came into class, we sat in a silent conspiracy to check out the new teacher. As teenage students, we always knew when we were getting a "bum" teacher. DIA had been sending teachers who could barely speak English, who believed that Indians were the scum of the earth (as related to them by DIA policy) and that Indian children needed to be saved from themselves.

Along came John, with his infectious smile and long hair.

He walked into the classroom with a guitar case and sat the guitar gently near the front of the class by his desk. He got us to interact with a game, played a song on his guitar, "Horse went around with his foot on the ground," and then read J.R.R. Tolkien's *The Hobbit*. We all knew that this teacher was going to be different. The girls of the class thought that John was the best thing since sliced bread. The boys were feeling apprehensive because John was initiating a softer side of male life in Alkali Lake.

Growing up on the rez was hard for all of us. On the weekends, my parents left the rez every chance they could. We did not stick around for weekend parties, but the following Monday in class I would hear how my classmates survived them. John made our classroom safe from the world of alcoholism and domestic violence. When we got to school, we were enmeshed in Bilbo Baggins' world of hobbits, and Gollum's "precioussss." John would do the voices, and we would sit and stare out our basement window into the skies, imagining that that world really existed. John's guitar did not stay dormant. Every day we would sing new songs and discover ourselves. Ian Tyson's "Four Strong Winds" and Cat Stevens' "Morning Has Broken" were my personal favourites from the songs that John sang for the class. Later on, we got a record player and brought records to school: Suzi Quatro, Chuck Berry, Bay City Rollers. But there was always an assignment attached to our listening:

"What does the song remind you of?"

"How does it make you feel, and why?"

"Would you do anything different? Why?"

John allowed us to express ourselves as students within the classroom and recognized us as members of the community.

Dad brought in Western movies for the kids to watch with

Lorne Dufour

parents on weekend nights. We prepared the popcorn for the movies as a class project and started to raise money for the Alkali Lake Youth Group. We wanted to travel—a dream that started in our classroom—and we did; for a class trip, we went to Fish Lake and stayed there for a week. There, John brought out his guitar and sang "There's a hole in the bottom of the sea." He was animated as he sang and we just giggled and shook our heads in silent admiration for him.

We were all excited to celebrate Halloween down at the lake. It was cold that night and it had snowed. Vehicles were few back then and the students rode on a hay wagon with open sides that was being pulled by the band tractor. I remember just concentrating on the fire by the lake to stay warm and think- ing that this would be fun. Alkali Lake Ranch wanted to "show off" to the reserve with fireworks. The owner of the ranch had already situated himself out on the water, about a hundred yards out. It was dark and windy and the ranch owner's boat tipped. John and Lorne swam out to see if they could rescue him. Lorne made it back to shore, and people attended to him quickly and took him away; but John did not come back out of the water. I do not remember the fireworks that night or even if it occurred. Parents were hanging onto their sons, the boys in class, to stop them from going out into the water to rescue our favourite teacher.

The next day, we did not have school. We had instructions from Chief and Council not to go down to the lake. Debbie and I tried to calm ourselves by playing records in the hall, but each song we played that John had listened to with us in class, just made missing him harder.

On behalf of our class in Alkali Lake, we are still waiting for John to return and we feel that John's spirit is here with us.

Jacob Roper

Acknowledgements

I thank my friend Harold Rhenisch for his patience and infinite help with this book. He is the editor and has been full of encouragement. I also thank Anne Walsh, who not only gave me my Olympia typewriter years ago but encouraged me to apply for a BC Arts Council writer's grant. The grant I received allowed me to step back from logging with my horses for a couple months and totally focus my energy into pulling this book together. I also thank the Museum of the Cariboo-Chilcotin for helping me while researching forty-year-old articles from the *Williams Lake Tribune*. I also thank Vici Johnstone of Caitlin Press, who has provided editorial help and who appreciated this book enough to publish it.

Tony Johnson, that great student of mine who always danced Indian-style down the street to school. Tony, I miss you. I wish you had survived to share the magic of your life with us.

Kelly, I understand that you were run over by a pickup driven madly through a rodeo ground where you lay, either passed out or asleep.

Kelly, we all miss you so very much. You were a great student and I was truly your student. Deno, Deno Chelsea, who was taken from us at such an early age, your intelligence and your leadership must help you in the spirit world. We needed you more than you needed us and it will be great to be together again.

Lastly, I thank my sweet wife Diana and my family for tolerating me for such a long time now, and for loving me.

I wish John was here to share so much of my life with. I loved him and he loved me. I wish Jacob was still big and strong and not an old man. I wish he could still carry me like a child and place me in a bathtub, as if I needed to be placed and needed to be carried. Sometimes people tell me not to believe some of the things Jacob tells me. Jacob, who has seen both sides of the clouds. Jacob, who lost his beautiful daughter. Jacob, who saved my life.

John, I send you my poems.

Already you have met our first horse, Prince.

Already you and Rose Marie are together.

Already, we miss you so much.

The Cariboo-Chilcotin

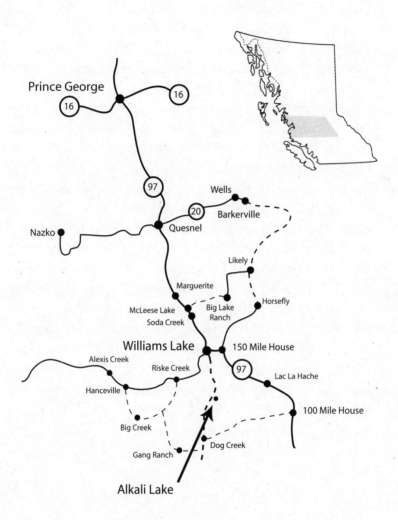

Prince George
16
16
97
Wells
20
Barkerville
Nazko
Quesnel
Likely
Marguerite
Horsefly
McLeese Lake
Big Lake
Ranch
Soda Creek
Williams Lake
150 Mile House
Alexis Creek
Riske Creek
97
Lac La Hache
Hanceville
100 Mile House
Big Creek
Gang Ranch
Dog Creek
Alkali Lake

A Note on the Author

Lorne Walter Dufour was born in Blind River, Ontario, on December 9, 1940. He attended the University of British Columbia, Simon Fraser University, the University of Ottawa, and Michigan State University at East Lansing. He met poets like Robert Duncan, Robert Creeley, Allen Ginsberg and the Canadian poet Red Lane, as well as the poetry teacher Peter Quartermain. His first marriage, to Joan Preston, gave him his son Adam in 1972. In 1975, he married his true love Diana Geensen, a librarian from Williams Lake, whom he met while teaching elementary school at Alkali Lake. Before moving to Alkali Lake, Lorne travelled with *Little People's Caravan,* a gypsy-style theater company with wagons pulled by magnificent Clydesdale horses. Lorne and Diana purchased a team of Clydes in 1976, Andy and Prince, and began logging with them near Salmon Arm, BC, where Lorne published his first book of poetry, *Spit on Wishes.* His second book of poems, *Starting from Promise,* won Broken Jaw Press's Poet's Corner Award in 2001. For over thirty years while working with horses and raising three children, Creole Dan, Tereina Marie and Easten Joe, Lorne has continued to write poetry, attend coffeehouses, and generously give his poems to the people.